500 YEARS
BEHIND
THE BLOCK

A personal history of R J Balson & Son

Richard Balson (signature)

RICHARD JOHN BALSON

Published by
Richard John Balson
West Allington
Bridport
Dorset

© Richard Balson 2014

ISBN 978-0-9931074-0-5

Printed by Creeds. 01308 423411 www.creedsuk.com

500 YEARS BEHIND THE BLOCK

This charming family history and memoir from Richard Balson harks back to a different age.

From the chaotic 'Shambles' in the 16th century to today's impersonal supermarkets, the story of RJ Balson & Son 500 years as England's oldest family business is a fascinating history of butchery and how it has changed over the years. In today's culture of the generic High Street it's heartening to know that there are still shops such as Richard's where traditional methods and local produce can be found.

Throughout the book Richard writes movingly about his family and the respect he has for them. Above all, this memoir reads as a wonderful tribute to his father.

Alongside the story of his ancestry, Richard gives life to his hometown of Bridport, a town full of characters and individuality. From his loyal customers to the local farmers, all are drawn with affection and regard. Richard's own charm and humour brings the personal touch to local history.

500 Years Behind the Block is told with wit and warmth from a true Dorset man –Enjoy the journey.

Frances Everitt
November 2014

Administrator of The Bridport Prize, 2002 - 2014
(International writing competition for short stories and poems)
Current owner of The Gables B & B and loyal purchaser of R J Balson's
wonderful sausages and bacon!

ACKNOWLEDGEMENTS

My sincere thanks to

Robert Crockford
Frances Everitt
Jane Tamone
for editing and proof reading

Stuart Broom
Keith Alner
Jim Rowe
for assistance with photographs

Allison Balson
for her patience during my dictation

DEDICATION

This book is dedicated to the memory of my father Donald Balson, who I had the pleasure of working alongside for over 40 years, and to all the family members over the last 500 years who have served from behind the block.

Donald Balson

CONTENTS

INTRODUCTION

In writing this book, I have attempted to take the reader on a journey from 1515 to the present day, discovering the history of the R J Balson & Son family in the butchery trade in Bridport, Dorset.

My personal memories date back to 1960, from living and working in West Allington and the relationship with my father. Some special customers and characters are mentioned as they are part of our story, which I hope will make interesting reading and give an insight into our butchery craft.

Reaching our Quincentennial anniversary is a remarkable achievement. The first time any British family firm has reached this milestone.

I hope this book is a suitable souvenir to mark this momentous occasion.

Richard John Balson

Bridport Town Hall

CHAPTER 1

IN THE BEGINNING

The year is 1515, King Henry VIII is on the throne in his seventh year as King of England. Robert Balson has been granted a shambles in the market town of Bridport. Robert, the founder of the Balson Butchery business wasn't to know that he had started a business that would still be trading in 500 years.

A milestone I'm sure he would have been very proud of. The exact date is Saturday 12th September 2015 and we will celebrate this occasion with a Quincentennial party at the Bridport Town Hall where it all began.

TRANSLATION OF 1515 SHAMBLES LICENCE

The indenture was made at Bridport on the 12th September 1515, between William Charde and John Orchard, bailiffs of the aforesaid borough on one part; and Robert Balson on the other part. They testify that the aforesaid bailiffs have granted and demised to the aforesaid Robert two shambles situated in the market of the town Bridport. Robert is to have and to hold the aforesaid shambles for the term of his life paying to the aforesaid bailiffs, and their successors in time to come, five shillings of legal money at the feasts of Easter and St Michael the Archangel (29 September) in equal portions and each Saturday during the year two pence and if it shall happen that the aforesaid rent of five shillings is in arrears for three weeks after the aforesaid feasts or if the aforesaid rent of two pence paid weekly shall be in arrears for a month then the aforesaid bailiffs and their successors shall have the reversion of the aforesaid shambles and the aforesaid Robert Balson shall be expelled, and the aforesaid Robert shall not alienate the shambles without a licence from the bailiffs of the borough under penalty of the year's rent on the shambles, and the aforesaid bailiffs and their successors lease the aforesaid shambles to the aforesaid Robert Balson for the term of his life according to the aforesaid terms.

By their warrant and against any claim that may be made by anyone else. In witness of this present indenture the parties have each put their seals.

Witnessed by William Preston, John Grauncell,
Robert Hasarde senior and others.

So in the beginning, animals were brought into the centre of all towns in England. Local farmers would bring their livestock in their horse and carts, or walk them into the shambles. "Shambles" was an open air market where animals were slaughtered and blood would drip into the gutter on the street, a messy scene. Life would have been very chaotic in the shambles; the noise and confusion of the whole operation must have been distressing for the public and the nervous animals.

The meat would then be cut up into large joints on wooden benches that were also called the shamble. These joints were sold to prospective customers to take home and cooked on an open fire as there were no ovens as we know them, or God forgive, microwaves. The joint would last all week, roast on Sunday, cold on Monday, stewed up for the rest of the week.

At this time there were no sanitary facilities or hygiene laws that exist today. But are we really surprised at how slaughtering and butchery was carried out at this time? Look at what was happening in our judicial system in England. Men convicted of high treason were hung, drawn and quartered i.e. emasculated, disembowelled, beheaded and quartered (chopped into four pieces). Then the remains were often displayed in a prominent place - let that be a lesson to you. Women were let off lightly; if they were convicted of high treason they were just burnt at the stake.

So, a very different macabre world in those days. These punishments were abolished in England in 1870. That's how it was, not very nice, but that was life in 1515.

Business in the open air shambles carried on until the town's rulers wanted to clean up this environment. Our own existing town hall was built on columns to accommodate the open market in 1785-6 at a cost of £2,000. This provided room to house thirty seven butcher stalls on the ground floor. Each butcher only had a two square metre stall to trade from.

The competition for business must have been frantic. The banter and noise from the butchers and customers must have made it a very hectic place to operate a business from. I would love to go back in time to experience the atmosphere in the shambles under the town hall. You could only trade in the shambles on a Wednesday and Saturday being market days, just as they are today.

Therefore, if you wanted to make a good living by selling meat you often had to have another job as well. The Balsons through the years ran some of the public houses in Bridport to sell their meat in the pubs to supplement their incomes. The Plymouth Inn, The Boot Inn, The Globe Inn, The King of Prussia, The Ship Inn, The White Lion, and The King's Arms were just some. It was not unusual for public houses to trade in both meat and beer, this eventually led to butchers shops trading six days a week.

ARTHUR BALSON

Arthur Balson was one of the last Balsons to trade at the shambles. Unfortunately he met with an untimely end. Arthur was the son of Henry and Elizabeth, with a stall at the market in 1852. He started a liaison with a Mrs Charlotte Wordsell. She had married her husband John Wordsell in 1848 when both were minors. John was a weaver who had been sentenced to nine months hard labour in 1859. The crime committed was larceny and the sentence of hard labour was to be served at the Dorchester prison.

Unusually for the time, Arthur and Charlotte were living openly as man and wife, a situation seemingly accepted by the community. Arthur was landlord of the Globe Commercial Inn in East Street, Bridport, he gave that up in March 1859 and the family, including Charlotte's son Tom, who called Arthur "father" moved to private lodgings at The King of Prussia, now The Lord Nelson.

Arthur struck up a guardian relationship with Tom and treated him as his own. He would play a game of soldiers with him, taking it in turns to pretend to playfully shoot each other.

On that fateful day of the 27th July 1859, the ten year old Tom pointed a shot gun at Arthur and pulled the trigger without realising it was loaded; Arthur died almost immediately. His funeral was attended by most of his fellow market butchers as well as other tradesmen. Around 100 in all attended his funeral which was held on a Sunday morning.

Taken from the archives of The Bridport News obituary July 30th 1859

The late Melancholy accident. The remains of the late Mr. Arthur Balson were interned in the Allington churchyard on Sunday morning last. A long procession, consisting of the principal part of the butchers attending Bridport market, and tradesmen, of the town, walked from the deceased's house to the place of burial.

A tragic end for 39 year old Arthur, but he will always be remembered and played his part in the Balson history. Who knows what might have happened if Arthur had not been killed? Maybe he might have left the business to his step-son Tom, as he had no children of his own, which could possibly have meant the end of the Balson name, but this did not happen and the business was carried on by his brother Richard after his death.

Richard was the landlord of The White Lion (now Tanners) and in 1865 became the landlord of The Boot Inn in North Allington, again they would have sold meat in the public houses.

In September 1874 he was still living in North Allington, this time in a house rented from Daniel Ewens Biddlecombe. He remained here until he took over their first shop in West Allington.

◆ ◆ ◆ ◆ ◆ ◆

CHAPTER 2

THE FIRST BUTCHERS SHOP IN WEST ALLINGTON

It was April 1887 and Richard Balson has the chance to open his first shop in West Allington by renting No. 7. The name Balson & Sons shown above the shop window.

Richard Balson stands proudly in the doorway.

In April 1890 Richard has the chance to buy the shop next door, 9 West Allington. Richard dies on the first of November and two of his three sons, Robert John Balson and William Balson take over the helm at No. 9.

Robert John Balson was trained as a butcher in the family business. In the 1880s he moved to Salway Ash and began to farm there. On the death of his father he returned to 9 West Allington to take over the running of the business with his brother William. He was living at New Close Farm, Dottery, where they had a slaughter room in one of the barns, giving them the control needed to produce their own meat. Robert John continued to run the business until the late 1920s.

His brother William died after a long and painful illness in 1927. He is

Christmas time.

buried in the St Saviour's Chapel in Dottery, Dorset.

Robert John retired in 1928 and was no longer involved in the business, which had been taken over by his nephew Richard John Balson junior (Pop), who paid £1,000 to buy the business, equivalent to £50,000 in today's money.

Pop had no money, but was lucky enough to borrow the money from his brother-in-law, Bill Spencer, and paid it back over a period of four years with the profits from the shop.

Robert John, having recently lost his brother and now retired from the business, began to suffer from depression. He was admitted to Herrison Hospital, a psychiatric hospital, in January 1929 and would have received extensive electric shock therapy, normal in those times. Nowadays you would have a good looking shrink lay you down and analyse you, stroke your hand and probe into your mind as to why you were feeling so low, and all this at an exorbitant cost.

He remained there for a year before coming out on licence. He was discharged on April 22nd 1930. Although his health was poor, it seemed that he had recovered. He was said to be cheerful and planning a holiday. Sadly this was all too short lived. In May 1930 he took his own life by cutting his throat. He was found by his sister Emma Selina Milverton, the widow of William Henry Milverton.

So, poor Robert John had retired, done his time, become depressed and took his own life, but with respect he has played his part in our family history.

Apart from a few alterations our shop at 9 West Allington is much the same today as it was way back then. However, in 1892 there was no glass in the window, it was an open fronted display with meat and carcasses hanging both inside and out. At night shutters were put up to close the shop up. In the winter it would have been unbearably cold in the shop. I know now when we get a north wind blowing through the open grills over the window just how cold it is. It is not unusual to be working in temperatures of 5 degrees in the shop and when you walk into the fridge and it feels slightly warm, you know it's cold outside.

In the winter months customers come in and say, "how do you stick the cold in here?" Well, you get used to it, put on more clothes and keep on the move. It makes our job a lot easier when it's cold. There's nothing worse than a butcher shop with the sun shining through the window. I'm thankful that being north facing we never get the full sun in our shop.

Whilst we are on the subject of temperatures, can you imagine a world without refrigeration? From about 1660 until 1950 ice was imported into Britain, cut from the frozen lakes of Scandinavia. Large lumps of ice would be delivered to the shop by horse and cart and be dragged down the passage to where the ice room was located. The ice enabled the meat to have a longer life. Modern household refrigeration came in around 1930, but they were big bulky fridges unlike the modern built-in fridges of today.

Before refrigeration, meat was kept in the larder. Almost every house had a larder built on the north facing wall (the coldest). Larger homes had a meat safe built into the larder. A wire mesh stopped flies and rodents getting in. Modern refrigeration is a must and makes our job so much easier. However, our modern fridges in the shop, and we have quite a few, (a big walk-in chiller, a big walk-in freezer, three chest freezers and four cool cabinets for the display of the fresh meat), are expensive to run. It all comes at a cost and with the motors running 24/7, our electric bill is huge. I'd go as far as to say, if we didn't have an electric bill to pay, we could be well off.

◆ ◆ ◆ ◆ ◆ ◆

FAMILY TREE

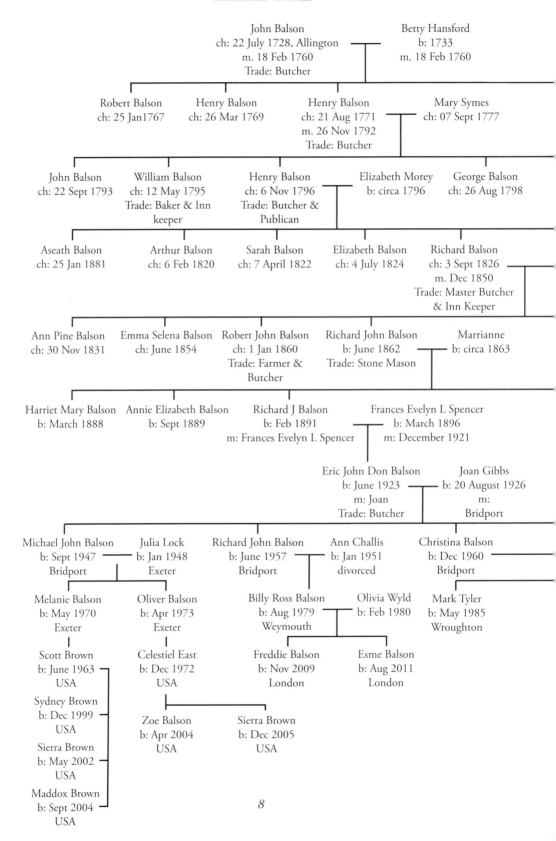

John Balson
ch: 22 July 1728, Allington
m. 18 Feb 1760
Trade: Butcher

Betty Hansford
b: 1733
m. 18 Feb 1760

Robert Balson
ch: 25 Jan1767

Henry Balson
ch: 26 Mar 1769

Henry Balson
ch: 21 Aug 1771
m. 26 Nov 1792
Trade: Butcher

Mary Symes
ch: 07 Sept 1777

John Balson
ch: 22 Sept 1793

William Balson
ch: 12 May 1795
Trade: Baker & Inn
keeper

Henry Balson
ch: 6 Nov 1796
Trade: Butcher &
Publican

Elizabeth Morey
b: circa 1796

George Balson
ch: 26 Aug 1798

Aseath Balson
ch: 25 Jan 1881

Arthur Balson
ch: 6 Feb 1820

Sarah Balson
ch: 7 April 1822

Elizabeth Balson
ch: 4 July 1824

Richard Balson
ch: 3 Sept 1826
m. Dec 1850
Trade: Master Butcher
& Inn Keeper

Ann Pine Balson
ch: 30 Nov 1831

Emma Selena Balson
ch: June 1854

Robert John Balson
ch: 1 Jan 1860
Trade: Farmer &
Butcher

Richard John Balson
b: June 1862
Trade: Stone Mason

Marrianne
b: circa 1863

Harriet Mary Balson
b: March 1888

Annie Elizabeth Balson
b: Sept 1889

Richard J Balson
b: Feb 1891
m: Frances Evelyn L Spencer

Frances Evelyn L Spencer
b: March 1896
m: December 1921

Eric John Don Balson
b: June 1923
m: Joan
Trade: Butcher

Joan Gibbs
b: 20 August 1926
m:
Bridport

Michael John Balson
b: Sept 1947
Bridport

Julia Lock
b: Jan 1948
Exeter

Richard John Balson
b: June 1957
Bridport

Ann Challis
b: Jan 1951
divorced

Christina Balson
b: Dec 1960
Bridport

Melanie Balson
b: May 1970
Exeter

Oliver Balson
b: Apr 1973
Exeter

Billy Ross Balson
b: Aug 1979
Weymouth

Olivia Wyld
b: Feb 1980

Mark Tyler
b: May 1985
Wroughton

Scott Brown
b: June 1963
USA

Celestiel East
b: Dec 1972
USA

Freddie Balson
b: Nov 2009
London

Esme Balson
b: Aug 2011
London

Sydney Brown
b: Dec 1999
USA

Sierra Brown
b: May 2002
USA

Maddox Brown
b: Sept 2004
USA

Zoe Balson
b: Apr 2004
USA

Sierra Brown
b: Dec 2005
USA

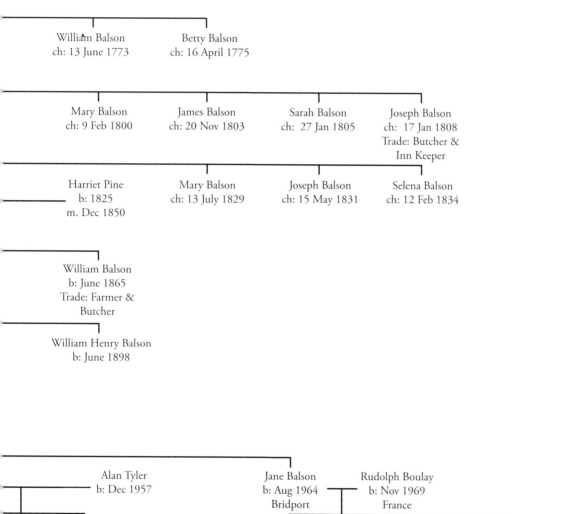

William Balson
ch: 13 June 1773

Betty Balson
ch: 16 April 1775

Mary Balson
ch: 9 Feb 1800

James Balson
ch: 20 Nov 1803

Sarah Balson
ch: 27 Jan 1805

Joseph Balson
ch: 17 Jan 1808
Trade: Butcher &
Inn Keeper

Harriet Pine
b: 1825
m. Dec 1850

Mary Balson
ch: 13 July 1829

Joseph Balson
ch: 15 May 1831

Selena Balson
ch: 12 Feb 1834

William Balson
b: June 1865
Trade: Farmer &
Butcher

William Henry Balson
b: June 1898

Alan Tyler
b: Dec 1957

Jane Balson
b: Aug 1964
Bridport

Rudolph Boulay
b: Nov 1969
France

Becky Tyler
b: Mar 1988
Trowbridge

Courtney Boulay
b: May 1995
Dorchester

Matilda Boulay
b: Feb 1997
Dorchester

Joseph Boulay
b: July 2001
Dorchester

CHAPTER 3

THE FAMILY AND EARLY YEARS

I was born in 1957, a very different world from today, living above the butchers at No. 9 West Allington, Bridport.

During opening hours it was a very noisy environment, thud, thud, the sound of the meat cleaver hitting the hornbeam butchers block echoing through the ceiling. There was no sound proofing between the ceiling and floor in the rooms above the shop, continuous noise and the conversation and banter of customers talking was always heard. I suffered from asthma as a child and when off school and lying in my bed, the noise from the shop was like listening to a radio. Then five o'clock came and there was silence. Father would come in from the shop, and we would have tea. In those days it was one o'clock dinner and five o'clock tea, regimentally so.

The shop used to shut from 1 to 2 o'clock, mother always cooked a splendid dinner, as you would expect with plenty of good quality meat around. My grandmother Frances Balson, better known as Queenie, also lived with us above the shop, her husband Richard (Pop) died when I was only four years old in 1961. I can just remember him waddling out to The Old Inn pub for a pint, where Miss Biles was the landlady. In fact my first delivery as a boy in the shop was taking the Sunday joint out to Miss Biles at The Old Inn, a cider pub. I would go to the Jug and Bottle, knock on the door and she would always give me a small glass of orange juice. I can still smell the cider now.

My grandmother Queenie worked in the shop. She would sit in the pay desk office, answer the telephone and dictate the orders to my father Don. She was a wonderful woman of many talents. There was nothing she couldn't do. Stern at times but with a heart of gold. If a button fell off your shirt, she would have it sewn back on before it could hit the floor. Darning socks, replacing zips, no problem, unlike today when it is all thrown away! She loved acting and singing, and was a keen member of the Bridport Amateur Operatic and Dramatic Society. She starred in many productions, such as Oklahoma, where she played Aunt Eller at the Palace Cinema in 1960. Her head for figures is what amazed me, she could add up so quickly. When calculators were invented, she did not trust them and always added the figures up herself just to make sure the calculator was correct.

She was a keen gardener and we had quite a large garden at the back of the shop which went right down to the river, this was her domain. Gran excelled in growing flowers and keeping the weeds at bay.

I went to Bridport County School and can remember crying my eyes out on the first day as I didn't want to go. Mother would walk us out there every morning about one mile and back again after school. We always walked with Betty Jones and her son Martin, who I soon became friends with and we attended each other's birthday parties.

MICHAEL BALSON

It was at this time that my brother Michael (10 years older than me) signed professional football forms with Exeter City FC. Father and I would go to every Exeter home match for the next ten years. There were some great highlights along the way, like the FA cup tie at home to Manchester United in January 1969, when Manchester were European champions.

I still recall the excitement of watching Best, Charlton and Law run out onto the turf at St James' Park. My brother playing against such footballing legends was wonderful. I know Dad was so very proud. A trip to White Hart Lane against the mighty Spurs followed in another cup tie, again such wonderful memories. Mike played 276 games for Exeter from 1966 to 1974. He then moved to South Africa, as lots of professionals finished their careers over there at that time. He signed for Highlands Park FC in Johannesburg and he played for them for five years with ex English league players Alan Gilzean (Spurs), Barry Bridges (Chelsea), Chris Chilton (Hull) and Alan Waldron (Burnley). They won the South African league during that time.

A riot after a league game made Mike think twice and Julia his wife along with their family decided to move to a safer haven, moving to America to play for The Atlanta Chiefs in 1979. Football was really taking off in America at this time, all the top European players were now ending their careers in the American league. Johan Cruyff, Pelé, Franz Beckenbauer, Gerd Muller, George Best, Rodney Marsh, Carlos Alberto, Alan Hudson, Alex Stepney to name but a few. Starring as centre forward for the chiefs was Jono Sono a big South African player who went on to manage South Africa in the 2002 World Cup.

Mike is now refereeing and coaching in the U.S.A.

CHRISTINA TYLER (NÉE BALSON)

I was a big tease to my eldest sister Christina; I can remember playing blind man's buff with her on the landing at the top of the stairs. I would blindfold her then spin her round a few times and point her in the direction of the stairs, then crash, and down she went, crying her eyes out to mother who gave me a telling off. I didn't realise how dangerous this was at the time and she hasn't let me forget it. Never did her any harm, it's all part of growing up.

This sort of excitement has all been replaced by playstation and computer games. Looking back now, I was probably a slightly cruel brother to my sister. I guess I liked to show off a bit to her and her friends, but that's normal behaviour for a brother surely. Christina had some attractive girlfriends and once I had passed my driving test I was given the job of giving them a lift home, because I was cheaper than a taxi.

Christina married Alan Tyler, a splendid chap, who could turn his hand to anything, very practical and an excellent do it yourself man. I was his best man when they married on 1st August 1981. He has turned out to be a great brother-in-law, although I don't see him as much as I'd like as they live in Bradford-on-Avon. Christina and Alan sail at Lyme Regis and they are very good at it, their trophy cabinet is full after winning almost every honour in the club. They have sailed in the fireball class in the English and European championships, finishing in the top six on most occasions and Alan went on to sail in the world championships and came sixth in the world.

Christina has run in the London marathon finishing in a creditable 3 hours 40 minutes. They now spend a lot of time helping out at their daughter's café The Teapot, in Bradford-on-Avon. A great place to eat, with of course Balson's award winning pork sausages on the menu. Their son Mark is very successful at everything he does and is now working for Sky TV and a keen sportsman - following in his parents' footsteps and another Manchester United follower.

JANE BOULAY (NÉE BALSON)

My younger sister Jane has followed in mother's footsteps as Miss Bridport. She is married to Rudie my French brother-in-law who is my partner in crime in the shop. Rudie makes all the sausages and being an ex-chef does all the cooking as well as offering tips and advice on cookery. This is available in both French and

English, with or without the odd swear word. Seriously, Rudie is an unbelievable worker, absolutely brilliant and irreplaceable. Customers love to wind him up when France lose to England at both football and rugby.

Jane is now in her 50th year but is still a party animal with many friends. She has a love of playing badminton, but has never managed to beat me. They have three children: Courtney has grown up to be a practical young lady, who can turn her hand to anything; Matilda an excellent singer with a beautiful smile (I'm going to be her agent when she is famous but for now she is a hard working student) and Joseph, Jane and Rudie's son is also studying and is cool and chilled out.

JOAN BALSON (NÉE GIBBS)

My mother Joan was a teenager when she witnessed James Cagney dancing at the Church House in South Street, Bridport. She was smuggled in by three American GIs who were staying with the family at St Michael's Lane during the war. This is a story that she loved to tell. Cagney was in Bridport entertaining the American troops. He was a fantastic dancer, I think mother is the only person still alive who witnessed his show. Obviously she has idolised him ever since.

It was around this time that she was voted the first Miss Bridport by the American GIs in 1940s. Mother's maiden name was Gibbs, along with brother Jimmy and the family they ran the famous St Michael's Lane bicycle shop. In those days everyone had a bicycle, now it's a car. You always remember your first bicycle and where you bought it, and most were bought at Gibbs' bicycle shop opposite the Hope and Anchor. My uncle Jimmy Gibbs was a comedian, a complete nutter and cracked jokes all the time, most of them were quick one liners. He was an RAF pilot in the war and flew over sixty missions on bombing raids to Germany in World War II. How he survived, I do not know. It was terrible to see only a few people at his funeral; he had served his country well and deserved a much better send-off. He was a war hero who put his neck on the line like so many who were not so lucky to come back, God Bless you Jimmy.

Mother's sister Betty married Douglas Eveleigh who was a fantastic gardener and grew onions the size of skittle balls and used to win many awards at Symondsbury Flower Show. They spent most of their married life at Valley View, Symondsbury, a pink Woolaways bungalow down a rickety path just off Sprakes' Corner. Unfortunately they were never blessed with any children. Betty was a wonderful person always with a smile on her face and a funny little giggle assisted by a glass or two of Lambrusco. She was the life and sole of the party.

Mother married my father Don in 1947. Mother likes to tell the story of how she first saw Don across the dance floor at the Drill Hall. He was dancing at the time with another woman. Mother went up to them, tapped the women on the shoulder and said, "someone outside wants to speak to you", and off she went and mother moved in on Don and that was the beginning of sixty-five wonderful years together.

On her wedding day, whilst in her wedding attire, a knock on the bicycle shop door saw a young lad standing there with his punctured tyre. Mother in her wedding dress, promptly set about mending it. That is family work commitment.

They were married and moved into their new home above the butcher's shop and went on to produce us four children.

Mother loved her pantomimes, starring in over thirty productions. She loved the camaraderie of the players, and Bernard Gale was the king, a fantastic man who did such a lot for the town of Bridport. My dad did not however enjoy pantomimes and never went to see mother in any of them. They had an agreement Dad never went to see mother in panto and mother never went to see dad play skittles. Ha ha!

DONALD BALSON

Dad, apart from passing his butchery skills on to me, was a keen sportsman. He played football for Bridport Thursdays, this was a team mainly made up of businessmen who shut their shops on Thursday afternoon, as it was half day, and played football.

A member of the Bridport Swimming Club, he loved the sea and was a great swimmer and great water polo player. Bridport had a very good water polo team in the late 1950s-60's, so good in fact that the whole team were selected to represent Dorset. They would often attract crowds of 500 or more spectators. They played in the river, nowadays health and safety would prevent this. It was not unusual for them to play and just 50 yards up the river there would be a dead calf or lamb that had strayed in and drowned.

Joan, Michael, Christina, Richard and Jane outside 18 West Allington, 1997

My father loved to socialize and played skittles for the swimming club skittle team, who won the Bridport Skittle league in their heyday. Some of the team members were: Cyril Travers, Teddy Rimmer, Cliff Broom, Stan White, Jack Down, John Miller and Jimmy Embon. They played their home games at The Boot Inn at North Allington, in the days when a young ginger haired Reg Lathey would stick up.

In 1969, Father was also the captain of the West Bay Skittle League, which I'm now a member of myself. It is a privilege and honour to follow in his footsteps.

It was at this time that Father enjoyed fishing, and purchased a sixteen foot clinker built wooden boat called Seapee in a 50/50 partnership with David Hine, a lovely man who owned Hine & Son printers in East Street. At that time The Bridport News was printed there (better known to locals as the whip whop). David sadly died early in life. After his death things just weren't the same and father sold his boat (David's funeral was the first I had ever attended).

I well remember a time out at sea with David and Father when our inboard engine broke down, and we had to row in during the most horrendous overhead thunder storm imaginable. The sea was flat calm, but it rained so hard that the rain drops seemed to bounce off the surface of the sea. I can remember being quite scared and was glad to reach the piers and the safety of the harbour. Then it was into the public bar at the Bridport Arms where the landlord was Bill Loud, a formidable character and a war hero. We would have a couple of pints while drying out. I remember on many occasions delivering meat to the Bridport Arms, and being met by Bill's two Alsatian dogs which were formidable as well.

Well that's a little about the family, now let's get down to the business.

◆ ◆ ◆ ◆ ◆ ◆

Bridport Swimming Club County Cup Winners 1958
G Meech, J Trevett, R Trevett, H Smith
J Gurd, D Balson, D Hoskins, A Latham, B Maddocks

Richard (Pop) Balson outside Symondsbury Church 1920

Delivery round in West Street, outside Fenwicks

CHAPTER 4

DELIVERIES

Early deliveries would have been done on the horse and cart or pony and trap. These modes of transport have served the Balsons well during the early years. Father used to say his first job when he was a boy was to be sent out into the field to catch the horse, so that the day's deliveries could begin!

How times have changed. My first job when I started work on a Saturday morning was to pump up the tyres on the bicycles so that the delivery could begin. Nowadays they just turn the key in the van. God they have got it so easy!

Just like refrigeration, it is hard to imagine a world without a motor car. It must have been very tough delivering to farms over unmade roads on the horse and cart, with no protection from the elements. No radio, no sat-navs, no mobile phones. How did they cope? I guess they were lucky to have the horse and cart, rather than have to walk. No need to worry about parking on double yellow lines, just somewhere to tether the horse was needed, and a good supply of manure for the roses was always on hand.

My father recalls the story of when his father "Pop" used to cycle to Lyme Regis on his bicycle without any gears, only to be rewarded when he got there with a bread and dripping sandwich, and my God was he glad of that! Bread and dripping now is supposed to be bad for you, but not if you are burning the calories off by cycling to Lyme Regis and back.

How many people do you know who drive their car to work when they could in fact walk or cycle? Then they sit down behind a computer all day, then they drive home, then they sit down and watch the television all night, and then they wonder why they are putting on weight.

From the 1960s we did our Saturday morning deliveries on the trade bike. We had four of these, four school boys and four meat rounds. One went north, one south, one east and I always went west. We must have been about thirteen. The other three boys employed at this time were: Alan Nichols, Nigel Challis and Nigel Toohill. The trade bikes were very hard to ride, no gears and the only way of getting up hill was the off the saddle manoeuvre, legs pumping and heart beating. I guess it kept us all fit.

Many businesses in the town used the bike as a delivery vehicle, before the motor bike and van were invented. We still have our delivery bike which sits proudly outside the shop as an advert. It can still be used and is in roadworthy condition, but nobody now seems to volunteer. Just lately it has been used for photo shoots, with customers taking pictures outside the shop to say they have visited England's oldest family business.

Nowadays, the door to door delivery has vanished. Years ago the butcher, baker, fishmonger, milkman and draper, would have a delivery round each week on certain days. They have been pushed out by the big multiples who sell everything and deliver, whereby you order your requirements online the day before.

Whilst we still do some private household deliveries, we mostly deliver to pubs, restaurants and hotels within a 15 mile radius. It's a shame really, delivering two pork chops to old Mrs Brown, down at the farm. I was quite possibly the only person she would see that day, she was so glad to see me and would talk the hind leg off a donkey, and I had a job getting away. But that's all part of the service, you might be asked to change a light bulb or open a jar of jam, post a letter or pick up something from the chemist, and you would do it with pleasure. Getting to know customers on a one to one basis, they become more than customers, they become friends.

My most memorable delivery was when I had just learnt to drive at seventeen, still young and innocent. It was a hot summer's day, I walked up the garden path and round to the back door, and there was my customer lying naked on her back sunbathing. Well, I didn't know where to look and I was certainly more embarrassed than she was. She grabbed a towel and covered her slender body, and invited me inside to pay me for my goods!

◆ ◆ ◆ ◆ ◆ ◆

CHAPTER 5

THE WAR YEARS AND RATIONING

Over the years we have survived many turbulent times: the plague, floods, fires, wars, and many recessions, but it must have been especially hard in the war years.

Price control and distribution of meat were taken over by the Ministry of Food on 15th January 1940, and rationing was introduced two months later, on 11th March. The idea of rationing was that everyone received the same quantity of basic food provisions on which to live and survive. However, in the meat trade such an equitable approach was difficult to define and enforce, and the majority of butchers had a tough time sharing out the rations. Meat rationing carried on for fourteen years ending on the 3rd July 1954.

I recall my father telling me that during the war we sold a lot of whale meat. It was sold under the name 'whacon' and was described as "corned whale meat with its fishy flavour removed." It was almost identical to corned beef, except "brownish instead of red".

A typical family meat ration for the week was:

1 pork chop

4 sausages

4 rashers of bacon or ham

1 egg

It's what I would eat for one meal in a good mixed grill.

I'm sure there would have been some black market or under the counter dealings going on, a little extra for the favourite customers. I know I would have succumbed to some arrangement.

My grandfather Pop enlisted in the Royal Navy on 15th August 1915, after initial training on the H.M.S Victory in Portsmouth he embarked on H.M.S Arlanza. She covered the Atlantic convoys in the northern waters around Britain. He served with her until December 1918, and was demobbed in January 1919.

After the war he was awarded the British war and victory medals, then he returned home to help run the family business when Robert John retired in the late 1920s. He married Francis Evelyn Louise Spencer (known as Gran and Queenie) at Branksome, Dorset on 20th November 1921.

My father Eric John Donald, known as Don, was called up for the Royal Navy during the Second World War, and he became a signal man on H.M.S Petard. H.M.S Petard was the only destroyer to sink submarines from the German, Italian and Japanese navy, and was also instrumental in capturing the Enigma files dossiers.

Father never talked about the war much, nor did he keep in touch with any of his ex-navy servicemen. I can only remember one occasion when a man, who had served with him on H.M.S Petard, called into the shop to see him. I think when the war was over, Father was only too pleased to get back to Bridport, back to work and normality.

◆ ◆ ◆ ◆ ◆ ◆

CHAPTER 6

SHOPS AND FRIENDS IN WEST ALLINGTON

When approaching Bridport from the west, our shop is now the first that you come to, but it was very different when I was a boy. Shops and businesses of different kinds were commonplace in the west end of town.

Over the years good customers and friendships were forged. Next door to us on our eastern side at No. 7 in the shop we once rented was Mr Ken Fudge the chemist. New mothers would take their babies to be weighed as well as purchasing the famous Fudges cough syrup known as "Fudges' Fire Water" a well known cure for the common cold, and just about everything else. It was a real old fashioned chemist shop with its own wonderful smell of antiseptic and iodine and plasters.

Down the alleyway called West End Row, was Steve Bishop's printers. They printed everything the old fashioned way on big printing presses, mostly hand operated, posters, programmes, raffle tickets and much more. Mr Bishop was a lovely man, I was always pulling his leg. He worked with his relation Bobby Davis, another local comedian. When the printers closed in the late 1960s the building was eventually purchased by Bridport Judo Club, who used it for their headquarters for many years; it is now a private house. On the other side of the alley was Underwood's cake shop and bakery.

The premises at No 5 were Indigo a ladies' fashion shop run by the lovely Denise Fussell. At No. 3 West Allington was Len Richards' jewellers shop, he had the job of winding the town hall clock for many years. When he retired Roger Snook took over the job.

At No. 1 West Allington was The White Lion public house, now called The Tanners. On the other side of our shop at No 11 West Allington was a newsagent. Previous owners include Lloyd Burwood, Ray Gilbert, Mr Barnard and Lou Morey who was a marvellous man with a good sense of humour. He liked to take the mickey just like myself that's why we got on so well. He opened at 5.30am daily, they sold all the things good newsagents do, and he was the king of verbal abuse in the best possible taste. Lou had a good team of paper boys working for him and one year they entered the paper boy under 16 five-a-side indoor football competion. One of the team members was my step-son Lloyd and they qualified for the finals at Wembley Arena. When we got to Wembley all the other teams seemed much bigger than ours and even had moustaches and beards, under sixteens? Anyway, they gave a good account of themselves and it was a great experience for the boys to have played at Wembley. It was a great shame when the newsagent shut and was sold for development and turned into five small houses.

I believe the local planners should have passed plans for flats above the shop and houses behind, but the shop should have stayed as a shop. We need our shops in Bridport, it's what makes our town special. With all the extra houses that have been built on the West Mead Hotel site and the Bartlett's site, the newsagents would have surely prospered. We miss the newsagents and the local banter.

The old Bridport industry building was turned into the Bridport Youth Hostel, and became a useful stopover for many a visitor, and now the hostel has turned into Bridport Foyer for waifs and strays from all around the country.

Moving westward was The Old Inn at 17 West Allington, run by the landlady Miss Biles. Samways bakery and cake shop were at 25 West Allington. The Rodber Hobby Shop was at 29 West Allington, every boy's dream. They sold balsa wood plane kits, dinky, corgi, matchbox cars and toys. It was a real arts and craft shop.

Mr Rodber died in the 1960s, his wife Joy kept the business going, eventually turning it into the Hobby Horse antique shop. She was a remarkable woman and a family friend. A very talented woman, who could make anything. She was involved with the Bridport Pantomime, making costumes and assisting with backstage makeup. Joy produced four lovely daughters, who are all very artistic. She sadly passed away in December 2013 in her 92nd year. Joy was always very well turned out and looked stunning for her age. She had been a customer in our shop for over sixty years and will be greatly missed in West Allington.

Just down the road at No. 46 was Bartlett's agricultural engineering works, they occupied quite a large site and employed a good number of staff. They came in very useful when parts of our mincer had to be repaired.

The boss man Hubert Bartlett was blind and he was looked after by Mr Cliff Castles, who was an employee of the firm. Cliff had done a lot for the town of Bridport, he was a very nice man, but unfortunately was a Manchester City fan. We had many great debates on football.

A little further on was Dennis Rawles grocers shop, and then at No. 59

was the Plymouth Inn that eventually closed in the 1990s. Miss Minnie Miller was the landlady, followed by Reg Brill and Barry Parkin, who was a fantastic landlord. Also at this time West Allington was home to most of the doctors and vets of Bridport: Dr Crawshaw, Dr Woodhead, Dr Cotterill and Dr Skellern all lived in West Allington and were all good customers of our shop. The two leading vets at that time were George Dickinson and Mr Marshall, who both lived opposite The Plymouth Inn.

In the later years two colourful characters who must be mentioned were John and Roz Higgins of the painted lady antique shop, which was housed at No. 5 West Allington. Roz was an eccentric woman, always dressed in purple and easily spotted in the town. John dabbled in all sorts of antiques and rented a garage from my father, which he turned into a workshop for restoring his furniture, the smell of French polish was divine.

So, with all these shops in West Allington, you never had to go past the White Lion bridge to do any other shopping. How times have changed!

◆ ◆ ◆ ◆ ◆ ◆

CHAPTER 7

LEARNING THE TRADE

Father taught me everything. It all began with skinning rabbits, an easy job unless you got an old tough buck rabbit, which was much harder to skin. In the old days you would save the rabbit skins as they were worth as much as the rabbits, posted off to a firm called Horace Friend of Wisbech, who would pay us for the pelts.

Unfortunately, nowadays they are all thrown away, a terrible waste. It is no longer fashionable to wear animal skins. Every week Lloyd Thomas from Salway Ash would arrive at the shop with fifty rabbits for me to skin. Lloyd was a game dealer extraordinaire; he would travel the West Country collecting game and deer from local shoots. He enjoyed a pint or two or three or four and could tell a good story, this has been inherited by his sons Steven and Simon, who are great company.

I recall an occasion when Lloyd pulled up outside the shop and I went out to bring the rabbits in. Opening the back of his transit van I noticed the floor of the van was nearly rusted out and littered with holes. "Blimey," I said to Lloyd "you're going to have to get a new van soon." Lloyd looked at me and said "No, no my son, you don't understand, when I go down to Exmoor collecting all the deer, all the blood runs out of the van on the way home." Well, there was a method in his madness I thought. He was a character make no mistake. I recall attending his funeral a few years ago, and his coffin was carried into the church by his six sons, with his loyal dog walking behind them, a lovely touch.

Of course, learning the trade and how to master the butcher's knife has its hazards, several scars on my fingers are reminders of careless slips. They say you only cut yourself with a blunt knife. This is true. When your knife is not as sharp as it should be, a bit more pressure to make the cut and whoops it slips and if your finger is in the way it's a visit to the first aid cabinet. It's all part of the job.

Dripping, now this is a messy job, given to the junior or newest member of staff to break them in. This was a good test for any prospective new butcher. You were not going to make it if you didn't want to get your hands dirty or greasy. Straight from the abattoir, large lumps of stomach fat had to be cut up small enough to pass through the mincer plate. Once minced it was into the clarifier to be rendered down. When heated up the fat turned into liquid, and when cool enough the liquid fat was strained and poured into greaseproof bags. It was important that the fat was not too hot otherwise the liquid would seep through the bottom of the bags, and not too cold otherwise it wouldn't pour. Then comes the worst bit, washing down the clarifier and emptying the dregs away. It seemed like you had to wash everything about three times to remove all the grease, the hotter the water the better.

Not so much dripping is sold these days, due to health reasons. Whilst we are on the subject of cleaning, Saturday is set aside for scrubbing everything down, all the trays, baskets, fridges, walls and floors all have to be cleaned thoroughly. The worst job was scrubbing the old cement floors, which had become quite dirty after a week's wear. We used to use caustic soda crystals, a very dangerous substance, to help remove the grease from the floor. Health and Safety would not let you use caustic soda today, fortunately we have a new tiled floor in the shop, which is much easier to keep clean these days.

Another messy job was preparing sheep's heads for customers who purchased them for their dogs. I recall a customer, Colonel Cantan from Eype, who would buy ten sheep's heads every week, which he would boil up for his dogs. There is a surprising amount of meat on the cheek of the head. My mother used to tell me that in the war, if they had a sheep's head stew for lunch on a Sunday, they were very lucky. How times have changed. Anyway, back to the head, they had to be chopped down the middle in half. One blow of a well-aimed cleaver did the trick, and this exposed the sheep's brain, a delicacy for the dogs. If your aim was not true you were in for a splattering of brain and skull. You soon learnt to hit the target every time.

Funnily enough, just after Easter this year, a lady came into the shop and said "This is the first time I have been in your shop for forty years." She went on to say she used to live in Bridport and her parents were customers and recalled they used to buy lovely chipolatas from us, and did we still sell them, I replied, "yes, the very same recipe of pork chips are right in front of you in the cabinet, Madam." She duly purchased some, and went on to tell me that she was Colonel Cantan's daughter. Well, how many businesses can tell a story like this. We spent the next ten minutes reminiscing about the past and in particular her memories of my father and his mother in the shop.

Chickens were bought in every week on the Thursday, ready for the weekend shopper. The chickens had to be drawn and trussed, that's gutted and tied down to those not familiar with butchers' terminology. At this time, two employees who stick in my memory were Fred Spiller and Gerald Tattershall, who were much older than me. They were full time butchers; Gerald in particular gave great service to our firm for over 30 years. Gerald also ran our Chideock shop in the 1980s, when we had two shops for approximately 15 years. He was a competent butcher and very popular with the customers.

Unfortunately, both Gerald and Fred have passed away. I remember taking Father to Gerald's funeral. Father himself was not very well at the time, but he wanted to pay his respects to someone who had given great service to the firm. He was glad he went.

At the end of the day scrubbing the block is hard work, back and forth with the "metal block brush" scraping the blood and grease off the top of the wood, applying pressure at the same time, your arms are aching and your back is breaking, back and forth you go.

The end result looks great, a clean block, the wooden grain showing through, looking its best again. A good hornbeam block should last a life time, if you look after it. By this I mean turning it over every now and then, and using different parts of the block, so as not to wear it in one place.

Some old blocks that you see in antique shops, which people buy for their old farmhouse kitchens, are terribly worn, but it gives it character and shows a lifetime of use. A good test is to place a marble on the middle of the block and see if it stays there.

THE PLUCKING MACHINE

In about 1995 we had the chance to purchase a plucking machine from a game dealer called David Ogilvy. He ran his business from his home near Cheddington. He wanted to sell up, and as we bought lots of pheasants from him, he gave us the opportunity to buy his machine. We met David to discuss it over a beer at the Winyards Gap pub in Cheddington.

We agreed a price for the machine, duly collected it and installed it in a shed in the garden at the back of the shop. The machine was very noisy and you had to wear ear muffs, but you could pluck about twenty pheasants per hour, as opposed to about four if you sat down to pluck them by hand. We kept the machine for about ten years, before we sold it on to another game dealer. During that time we processed thousands of pheasants on it.

Times have changed and we now sell more pheasant breasts than whole birds. This is because the breasts can be pan fried in about five minutes depending on the heat of your pan and size of the breast, compared to roasting a whole pheasant with all the trimmings which would take about an hour. Customers want quick easy meals these days. At this time we were buying straight from the shoots, we would take everything they shot at Chideock Manor, which was owned at that time by the Weld family. They were good customers; we were both happy to barter the value of the pheasants against their monthly meat bill, this proved to be a good way of doing business. We were selling a lot of pheasants in the feather in the mid 1980s, ten pheasants for £10. In fact we are still selling them for the same price thirty five years on, no inflation here. There is now no value in the pheasants in the feather. The shoots make their money on the guns. The value is in the labour to prepare the pheasants, but times have changed and customers do not want to prepare them themselves any more.

They say food is expensive, but not if you are prepared to put some time and effort into it. Take a 25 kilo bag of potatoes costing £6, how many meals can you get out of that? Our world today sees the supermarket selling ready peeled potatoes, covered in goose fat, in a disposable baking tray. So easy for the housewife, just bang the tray in the oven and when cooked no washing up, just throw the tray away, but it all comes at a cost.

AXMINSTER MARKET

On Thursday afternoons Father would drive down to Axminster some 12.5 miles away to visit the livestock market and buy his animals for the week. The auctioneer was Mr Frank Rowe, a larger than life character known to all, a very popular man who became a great friend of Father's. Father would always take Frank down some sausages and loved to get paid in verbal abuse around the auctioneering ring. The market was a great meeting place for farmers, buyers, and butchers, with a fantastic atmosphere.

As a result of Frank and Father's friendship many skittle matches were arranged between the Axminster butchers and the Bridport butchers. In those days all the local butchers went to the market to buy their animals and great friendships and rivalries were formed, and many great skittle matches were played.

Axminster Market 1969.

Frank Rowe Auctioneer on the left, Donald Balson second right

Unfortunately, Axminster Market closed in 2006 and now all the buying is done over the phone. At least we are using the same slaughter house, C. Snell of Breeches Farm, South Chard, Somerset. We have been doing business with them for over 50 years, another great family business offering locally sourced meat with traceability from the farm to the fork.

❖ ❖ ❖ ❖ ❖

CHAPTER 8

LEAVING SCHOOL AND THE FAMILY HOME

In 1972 my father purchased Stoke Lodge No.18 West Allington for the sum of £18,000, a lot of money at the time.

This was the first time since 1890 that the Balson family had not lived over the shop. Stoke Lodge was a very large house, in fact it was the first house to be built in West Allington and like all old houses it had plenty of character and needed plenty of maintenance over the years to keep it together. A lovely family home, plenty of big rooms, great for entertaining especially at Christmas when we would always have more than twelve around the table. Mother had her Auntie May Allen (former landlady of The Anchor Inn, Burton Bradstock) come live with us and she looked after her, and Father had an en-suite added to the downstairs front room. Mother deserved a lot of credit for looking after her and nursing her in her final days, until she passed away in the front room at Stoke Lodge in 1975.

I went on to Colfox School, where I stayed on in the upper sixth and got O level grade 1 at Woodwork, making a guitar, which I still have today, for my project. Alas I cannot play the guitar, I'm not really musical, I would love to be able to sit at a piano and belt out a tune, but this will never happen as I don't have the time or the patience to play. I also got O level Mathematics which has been very useful in the shop. I always knew I was going to come into the business; it was just a matter of when. I could have left school after the 4th form, but decided to pursue my interest in sport etc… After all, they say the best days of your life are at school, I think they are right, you just don't realise it at the time. I left school at 17 years old and entered the big world of working full time.

In the evenings, Father would often cross the road to The Plymouth Inn for a couple of pints, and why not? He worked bloody hard. The landlord at the time was Barry Parkin, who was a jovial man, one of the best landlords ever and a good customer too. Barry was a chef by trade, and became one of the first publicans to offer good quality food in pubs. The Plymouth Inn became very popular and soon had football and cricket teams, as well as darts and table skittles.

There was a time when I was playing football for the school on a Saturday morning, for Bridport Reserves in the afternoon and the pubs league on a Sunday morning. It was three games in 36 hours, but that was when I was young and fit. These days professional footballers moan about playing two games a week. Ridiculous!

It was about this time in my life when I was admitted to Weymouth Hospital to have my appendix removed. After several stomach pains and a thorough examination, I was on the operating table. However, my appendix had burst, and I now had peritonitis and the poison from the appendix had leaked out over my intestines. A thorough mopping out job had to be done, leaving me with a 10 inch scar across my stomach. This really knocked me back and I was very ill for a number of weeks, losing about three stone during my time in hospital; however, I count myself lucky as some people have died from this in the past. After a couple of weeks they sent me to Portland hospital to convalesce. There, I was put on a ward with motorbike accident victims. I was surrounded by patients with broken arms and legs all bandaged up and suspended from the ceiling at every angle. This experience put me off motorbikes for life. It took me about six weeks to fully recover and get back to work and enjoy my sport again. I was back playing football for The Plymouth Inn, Paul Young would run down the wing and send over a perfect cross for me to head the ball into the net, great memories for me.

It is hard to believe, but I was very shy as a youngster. However, during my Colfox days I matured in many ways. At nineteen I got married to my first wife Ann Challis, who had a son Lloyd and a daughter Stephanie from a previous marriage. Ann was the daughter of Vic Challis of the Challis Brothers building firm. They were excellent builders and have left many buildings to remind people of their work.

We bought 9A West Allington, a small house down the passage behind our shop. Ann fell pregnant, and it was during this time that we experienced a horrible time in our lives. It was June 3rd 1979, my birthday, and Bridport had a spell of torrential rain and bad storms. The rain continued and a lot of the low lying ground was flooded. We were hit by a double whammy, when the river burst its banks at St. Swithun's Bridge, the water rose from two inches to two feet in seconds. It was like a tidal wave coming across the road straight at the shop. The water was level with the letter box in the shop, even deeper in our recently purchased new home; there was nothing we could do. I can remember looking at my front room, three feet deep in dirty water, I just cried. We went over to live with Mum and Dad at Stoke Lodge until the water went down and the clean-up could begin, both in our home and shop.

Richard Balson West Allington Floods 1979

Our son Billy arrived on August 31st 1979, a joyous day. I was at the birth and again cried my eyes out, I'm not ashamed to admit it. What a moment and what a size; Billy weighed in at almost 10lb! Billy was always big and strong for his age; I put it down to all that marvellous meat.

We sold number 9A because it was slightly damp for bringing up a young child and moved in above the shop, which had been empty since Father had bought Stoke Lodge.

Billy's first day at Symondsbury School turned out to be a day I would never forget. Gran was very ill but wanted to see Billy in his new school uniform on his first day of school. Gran saw him on his way to school, but that was the first and only time, as she passed away peacefully that afternoon, in the same room as Auntie May at Stoke Lodge. She had a wonderful life and had given so much time to the business, unpaid I might add. A true family great, never forgotten, there will always be a photo of her in the shop, and when the older generation come in they often reminisce about Gran sitting at the pay desk. I still miss her now.

Times were changing and most shops in Bridport were staying open during the lunch hour. So it was about this time we decided to stop closing for lunch and stayed open between one and two o'clock. We also moved our half day from a Thursday to a Monday. This made more sense as Monday is always a quiet day after the weekend, and we can do more work on a Thursday afternoon, which is more beneficial to us as the weekend looms. Our new opening hours were 7am-4pm without a break, so if you wanted lunch you had to eat on the run. Customers' eating habits were changing too, and we were introducing more exciting varieties of sausages to meet the customer demand: wild boar; duck and orange; venison; pork and leek were going down a storm, up to twenty different varieties.

The appearance of the supermarket has been a threat to small businesses all over the country, and has completely devastated some town centres. Bridport is very lucky to have so many independent shops and a thriving market, keeping our town alive. It is amazing that Bridport still has three butchers' shops, although I can remember when there were seven.

My father could remember five butchers' shops in Lyme Regis. Now there are none. All gone. So sad. You would have thought one shop could have made a decent living there. We are surviving by offering a personal shopping experience with great local products and great customer service, making shopping in our shop a pleasure. Entertaining customers, telling them a bit of gossip, and what we don't know we just make up, all in the best possible taste.

THE OLDEST

It was June 1984, Basil Short the Bridport local historian, had been doing some research on our family. He had traced us back to being butchers in Bridport since 1535. Wow… there must be some mileage in this I thought. I wrote to the governing body of butchers, through their trade paper the Meat Trades Journal. I put the proposition to them that R J Balson & Son est.1535 could be the oldest family butchers in England. The Meat Trade Journal wrote an article asking their readers if anyone could beat this claim. The answer came back. NO. You can say you are England's oldest family butchers – this was great news.

We received lots of publicity and had new stationery printed by Mr Creed the printer to advertise our new claim to fame.

◆ ◆ ◆ ◆ ◆ ◆

CHAPTER 9

SPORT AND LEISURE

I always had Saturday afternoon off, to play football for Chideock FC in the Dorset league. Our home pitch was in Symondsbury and I so enjoyed my amateur footballing days. I have so many great memories of playing for Chideock, and made some great friends along the way. I consider myself to be fairly good at that level, very good in the air. I used to jump so high that I suffered from altitude sickness ha ha…

In 1982 my brother Mike was home on holiday and I got him to turn out for us in a league game, against Stadium of Portland, this was a great occasion for me. The only time I have played 90 minutes alongside my brother in the same team.

We enjoyed a fair amount of success in the Dorset league, and our best season was in 1988 when we won the league and cup double. Playing in the Dorset league took us to all parts of the county, to towns and villages I would not otherwise have visited, and left many happy memories.

Chideock, Champions of Division Three (South West), and Winners of the Division Three and Four (South West) Cup. Back Row (left to right): Ian Pidgeon, Kevin Davies, Brian Kick, Colin Willcox, Mark Bevis, John Challis, Billy Balson, Jim Wrench (Manager/Physio). Front: Phil Chard, Sean Day, Andy Harrison (Capt), Patrick Tuck, Mark Broad, Kevin Challis. Mike Challis and Paul Young were also regulars throughout the season but are not pictured.

One particular fixture saw us playing away at Sturminster Marshall; I was driving my car taking three other players and went to Sturminster Newton by mistake. Realising our error we went on to Sturminster Marshall only to arrive twenty minutes late. The rest of the team were not very happy with me and they have never let me forget my unfortunate mistake, as they were two nil down when we arrived.

On another occasion an away fixture at Gillingham, I was mucking about in the pre-match warm up and decided to jump up and spring the cross bar. Little did I know that the bar was only resting on top of the posts on a four inch spike? The bar sprung up and came off and came down and hit me on the head, driving my top incisor through my lip, all this before the game! A lump the size of an egg came up on my head, and after the necessary medical attention and mandatory piss taking I spent the whole game playing on the left wing, so I wouldn't have to head the ball. I honestly don't think many players would have carried on after that, and these days they would have gone to hospital and probably been detained overnight. Once again, my team mates never let me forget this incident, but it was my own fault.

We had a good team at Chideock, but more than that, a great team spirit and a fantastic social side, with lots of great fund raising events. In the summer of 1987, whilst on the golf course, I said to the current Chideock manager Mr Kelvin "Basher" Dawe, "we're going to have a Grand Fete this year to raise some money." It was one of my better ideas – we have run the Symene Sports Club Fete (Symondsbury Cricket Club & Chideock Football Club) every August Bank Holiday since, and it's now in its 28th year.

The fete raises much needed funds to keep the club house solvent and to support local charities. It has grown into Dorset's biggest fete and is a tribute to the team of helpers and sponsors, who all contribute to the success of the event, raising thousands of pounds along the way. The fete is the highlight of the Symondsbury social calendar, attracting over five thousand visitors each year from all over the country.

I have always been interested in all aspects of sport and have an interest in sports quizzes. I remember listening to "Brain of Sport" on the radio, and was always amazed at the extent of knowledge the contestants had.

A 'Question of Sport' was, and still is, one of my favourite TV programmes, David Vine and David Coleman being excellent quiz masters. I myself have had a fair crack of the whip asking questions. I organise the annual Chideock Football Club Sports Quiz, better known as the prestigious Clinker Shield, which is an old toilet seat covered in the previous winners' names. The quiz was hosted at various venues: The Ilchester Arms, The London Inn, the Leisure Centre and since 1992 it's been held at the Symene Club House in Symondsbury.

I very much enjoyed being the question master and did this for a period of 25 years. I had a lot of fun compiling the questions each year and always liked to add the odd trick question. Two of my favourite questions are:

1. How many legs are there on a snooker table?
Answer: None, they are all underneath.
2. In which sport did Christmas Day fall on Boxing Day?
Answer: Horse Racing.

The quizzes were always very competitive and a good social sporting evening was enjoyed by the 32 teams. We had a lot of fun during those November Sunday nights at the club house; the most successful team winning the Clinker Shield on many occasions was the Beaminster Social Club team, led by Nigel Walters, a true mastermind of sporting knowledge.

Now that we are all too old to play football, we play cricket in the Crosby Cup under the name of Chideock Vets. This is a handicap evening league cricket competition. We are not very good but have a great time, taking the mickey mostly out of our own team, but also out of the opposition. It is sometimes good to play sport for fun and not to take it too seriously. However, we have won the evening knockout on a couple of occasions.

I also play golf at Bridport and West Dorset Golf Club, according to Mark Twain, a good walk spoilt. I don't see it that way. Golf is a great game, but very frustrating at times. I have played a lot of golf with two of my best friends George G T Brown and Andrew Harry Harrison, my next door neighbour.

George is a Scotsman with short arms and deep pockets, he's as hard as nails, but has a heart of gold. You would certainly want him next to you in the trenches. Harry is an Englishman but doesn't look English, if you know what I mean. He is a great friend to me and I will never forget the compliment he gave to me about my father one day. Unfortunately, Harry's father died when he was quite young

A winning team, Harry, George and Richard

and he never got to know him. When my father passed away, I was obviously feeling very low, and Harry said to me that if he had known his father, he would have wanted him to be just like mine. I will never forget that.

Anyway, George, Harry and I all play off similar handicaps, and we have had many battles on the golf course; we are all great competitors. None of us likes losing to one another, whether we are playing for a pound or just a tee. Also, we all enjoy laughing at each other's downfalls. When Harry is in a bunker, and he is still in there four shots later, George and I are killing ourselves with laughter. Then there was the time when I lost my footing and slipped down a muddy bank – I went down, the trolley tipped up, the clubs and balls all came out and were covered in mud. I looked up, hoping in vain for a little sympathy, but I should have known better, George and Harry were laughing their heads off. That's what friends are for.

Every now and then, one of us would play really well, clean up and take the money and be on a high for the rest of the day, but over the year the money went round. After a hard week at work it's nice to have a round of golf. If the weather is nice, it's even more enjoyable, and if the putts drop it's even better.

FATHER-SON COMPETITION

When my son was growing up, he played football for the Junior Bees' Football team. A really nice bunch of lads managed by Steve Scrummy Gale, and they were very successful, winning their share of trophies.

As Billy grew into adulthood, we enjoyed our sparring and individual duals on a father and son basis. Pride was very much at stake, and I did not want to lose to my youthful and fitter son, and Billy didn't want to lose to his more experienced and older father. I was carrying some twenty years and four stone, which is not easy in any competition. We enjoyed very competitive and aggressive squash matches with neither Billy nor I giving an inch. Both sweating like pigs you could literally wring out our shirts. Honours were pretty even, taking it in turns to be the victor and gloat for the evening.

Then came the big one, the Super Stars TV challenge. We both chose five sports to play against each other. So I chose sports that I thought I could beat him at – tennis, badminton, snooker, squash, darts and I just about did; Billy chose swimming, sprinting, long jump, triple jump, throwing a cricket ball and he won all his events. This meant we were five wins each, so had to settle for a penalty shoot out to decide a winner. We travelled over to Symondsbury football pitch accompanied by our neutral referee Mr Brian Kick, who was lodging with us at the time. Brian was my best man, as well as being one of Billy's godfathers. Ten penalties each. I won the toss and went first and to my amazement managed to score 10 out of 10 penalties with Billy in goal. Then we changed around and I went in goal to face Billy's 10 penalties, he scored the first three and then missed the next one and the competition was over. It is only fair that I occasionally remind him about this.

SKITTLES

Playing in the Bridport Skittles league for the Swimming Club, the league's oldest team which started in 1947, I remember a game that was played at the Toll House in East Road. It was a very cold winter's night, so cold in fact that everyone kept their coats on, and only had one pint each to drink.

That night three balls from Barry Pearce have remained in my memory to this day, first ball…popper, second ball…popper, third ball…flopper (in skittles terms 0-0-9) a very unusual throw; I have never seen it happen again.

Another game which is engraved in my memory was a game against the TT lads at The Boot Inn, North Allington. Tom Cox was a big man with a personality to match and not a bad skittler was known all over Bridport. Tom was the proprietor of Cox's Corner, second hand furniture dealer in St. Michael's Lane, as well as other business ventures. This particular night, Tom was on good form, and was very good company. The trouble is, he had had rather too much to drink, stumbled and fell over on the alley. It took the whole of Tom's team to get him back on his feet. Such a laugh, such a great character, everyone will have fond memories of Tom Cox.

SYMONDSBURY MUMMERS

In 2007 I was invited to join the Symondsbury Mummers, a group of men, with connections to Symondsbury parish. The invitation to join was to take George Pigeon's place, who had recently died. I could not refuse; it was an honour to follow in his footsteps. George was known as Mr Symondsbury. He was a wonderful man and a great sportsman loved by all, and he knew so many people, being an ex-postman.

So I was also following in my mother's footsteps in acting the Mummers' play. In Victorian times Mumming plays and groups were common throughout southern England. Now only a handful survive, performing to original scripts.

Foremost amongst these is the Symondbury Mummers' play. Their Play is considered to be the most complete example of this kind. I play the part of the Egyptian King, strangely the same part once played by my uncle Douglas Eveleigh in the 1950s. The play has the theme of death and resurrection, and is typically performed at the end (death) of the old year – and the start (birth) signifying the beginning of the New Year.

I introduce St. George the hero of the play, he fights four bold warriors, Captain Bluster, General Valentine, Colonel Spring and the Gracious King. St. George kills them one by one and summons the noble Doctor, who resurrects them with his magic potions. All good fun, a great bunch of blokes giving entertainment to generations of families.

We visit fetes, pubs, residential homes, WI Christmas parties or any organisation wanting some traditional entertainment around Christmas time. Our services come free, but we are grateful for some bread and cheese, a cup of tea or a glass of mulled wine and a mince pie, then we pass the hat around for a charitable donation.

◆ ◆ ◆ ◆ ◆ ◆

CHAPTER 10

BALSON'S BANGERS HIT THE STATES

In September 2007 my brother Mike and his son Oliver starting selling sausages on-line in the U.S.A. After much consultation and discussion recipes were replicated and the R J Balson and Son brand expanded across the water. Trading also as England's oldest family butchers carries a lot of credibility in America, as we are older than the country itself.

There are thousands of ex-pats living all over the States craving English bacon and sausages. In 2009, bacon was also introduced to the U.S market. In 2011 they expanded, making chipolatas, then a year later beef and horseradish was added to the range. The ex-pats love the English style bacon now available to them, as the American style bacon is all streaky. The business has been growing slowly for the past seven years. The sausages and bacon are made in Texas. Oliver processes the orders and they are shipped out all over the U.S.A via courier. However, they do things slightly differently in America The sausages are made, then steamed and then instantly frozen. When sold, customers only need to brown and serve as they are already cooked. Take a look at the American website www.balsonbutchers.com. It is quite amazing that Ruth Thomas, daughter of Lloyd Thomas mentioned earlier in the book, is one of Balson's U.S.A customers in California, where they run an English style pub.

In June 2009 Allison and I flew to New York to help Mike and Oliver run their trade stand at the Fancy Food Show in the Jacob Javits Convention Centre. I guess this was Balson's first international convention, and what an eye opener. This turned out to be quite an experience. As it happened, the day we arrived Michael Jackson had died. It was unbelievable. Memorabilia on every street corner and emotional women crying everywhere. The news on TV and the papers dominated the story of his death.

It was so busy. I personally didn't like New York. It was like walking in a football crowd everywhere you went. I'm not used to that volume of people. They say it's a City that never sleeps and my word they are right. We spent three days helping at the exhibition, cooking samples and promoting the products. It was a great experience for us, and great for Mike and Oliver to have us on board.

They had lots of enquiries and leads to follow up on after the show, so it was a great success, and it was the first time I had been on a business trip overseas. One particular conversation with a man from Texas stays in my mind. We were talking about the sausages and he commented on how strange and funny my Dorset accent was. He was beginning to take the mickey, but I came back with one of Father's all-time favourites by saying "you know what makes the grass grow in Texas" and he replied "what's that?" I said "Bull Shit"! He thought that was great and we had a good laugh.

◆ ◆ ◆ ◆ ◆ ◆

Left to right Oliver Balson, Richard Balson and Michael Balson

CHAPTER 11

BUILDING VALLEY VIEW

In 2004 I met a wonderful woman called Allison, she is my soul mate. We are so alike, we think and say the same things. In 2008, after a long and expensive legal battle, my divorce came through to end a very difficult time in my life. Allison and I were living together at West Bay Road, when my Auntie Betty Eveleigh (Mum's sister) died. She lived in a Woolaways bungalow in Symondsbury. I owned a third of the property, the other two thirds owned by my sister Christina and her husband Alan, and Jane and Rudie.

We sold our West Bay home, enabling us to buy my sisters' shares from them, and we went to live with my mother and father at No 18 West Allington. This was a great experience. They were getting older, and appreciated the help and assistance we gave them while we were there, and it was great to spend some quality time with them. I had forgotten just how cold the old house was, as there was no central heating.

We got plans approved to demolish the old bungalow and build a new house. We bought an old dilapidated caravan to put on site for the builders, just so they would have somewhere dry to have a cup of tea during the build. We became very attached to the caravan and spent most weekends living there, so we were more hands-on at weekends to help with the build.

After several quotes, we chose Neil Crabb construction to build the house, a fantastic firm. Neil is an excellent builder, who was happy to let us help with the project whenever we could, to help keep the cost down. Before Neil started on the build, we had to knock down the old bungalow. Our architect told us it could cost up to £10,000 if we were to get a firm in to knock it down and to take it away. Blimey, I thought, that's a lot of money. We had to have a drive way put in, so we got a digger to take two feet of soil out for the drive way. Then Allison and I set about taking the roof tiles off and putting them in the driveway for hard-core. Then we knocked out all the partition walls from the inside, hiring a skip for £250.00 to get rid of all the plaster board. The rest of the stud walls were burnt, with the best timbers saved for the garden fencing. Next we took the roof off, again saving the best timbers for fencing. This just left the chimney and the walls. The walls were two feet wide, cement panels made on the old Woolaways site at West Bay (now Meadowlands). The panels were bolted together; one by one we took them down and placed them in the driveway. Everything got recycled except the old double glazed windows that we had to take to the dump; two skips were required at a total cost of £500. The site was cleared and the builders moved in. Allison and I had knocked the whole bungalow down manually saving £9,500 in the process. Not bad when we did this over a period of two months, in our spare time as we both had full time jobs. All with just a variety of tools, and hard graft, but it was both rewarding, fulfilling and saved us a lot of money.

The build started on 1st March 2010. We had a good summer that year, the weather was kind to our builders and we helped whenever we could. Once the shell was up and the roof went on, the plasterers, plumbers and electricians moved in. We finished the second fix ourselves, completed all tiling on both the walls and floors, all the painting and staining. We also fixed all door frames, hung all interior doors, fixed all the skirting boards and laid all the oak flooring throughout, finally fitting the kitchen and worktops to completion. Being able to do this ourselves saved a huge amount of money and kept the build on budget.

I must pay tribute to my Allison, who helped throughout in every aspect of the build. Not being sexist but she is as good as any man at DIY that you will ever see. She loves nothing better than having a power tool in her hand. How many women do you know who want a chain saw for their birthday? But I won't let her have one. She routed out all the door architraves, and was such a tremendous help. I couldn't believe my eyes when one day Allison climbed into the digger which had been left on site, started it up and proceeded to remove a tree stump under the supervision of our neighbour Darrel Beadle. How many women would do that? I must admit I was worried about the glass greenhouse.

We moved in on Christmas Eve 2010. The build took nine months. There were still a few things to finish, such as carpets and flooring, but we managed with cardboard on the floor, until we could afford what we wanted. We are now blessed with a fantastic home, which we helped design and build and Auntie Betty is always in our thoughts.

◆ ◆ ◆ ◆ ◆ ◆

Richard and Allison's new home

CHAPTER 12

CUSTOMERS AND CHARACTERS

Over the years many loyal customers and great characters have come and gone. Here are some of my favourite memories of strange occurrences and coincidences about people whom I have been privileged to have known.

The Rep

It was a Friday morning in the mid 1980s. Friday mornings were very busy. A rep called Tony always used to call in selling cooked meat products. He was an old fashioned rep, who liked to tell a story and a joke or two. Father did not like him calling on such a busy morning, and saw him as wasting my time. Anyway one day Father had had enough and told Tony not to call ever again.

A couple of weeks went by and we never saw him, just as Father thought he had seen the back of him, he called again. He was talking to me at the end of the shop (wasting my time). Unlike Father he lost his temper, the only time I have witnessed this in forty years. He picked up his long steak knife, approached the rep, pulled out his tie from inside his jumper, cut his tie off, thrust it into the rep's chest and ranted "I told you never to come into my shop again!" The rep turned and fled out of the door very quickly. We never saw him again. Father was very pleased with himself, and the story always brought a smile to his face whenever it was mentioned. This act of aggression was totally out of character for Father.

Mr John Jowitt

Mr Jowitt from Brook House Chideock was a well-known local artist. A true gentleman, dressed impeccably, would always tip his hat to the ladies and say good morning, so polite and well mannered.

He once told me the story, that when he was studying at the London School of Art as a student, he used to drive an open top red sports car. In those days you could park anywhere in London, leave the top of the car down, leave goods on the back seat, leave the car unlocked, go off and return a few hours later and nothing would have been touched. Now, in the modern world they would pinch the car lock stock and barrel.

In 1985 we commissioned John to paint a picture of Father in the shop, as we thought it would make a nice Christmas present. It cost £75. All the family chipped in and we presented it to him on Christmas Day. I remember it took three sittings. The painting now hangs in the shop and Father is looking over us. Mr Jowitt was a well-known artist, who has left many paintings to be remembered by. He was a good customer in our Chideock shop and I fondly remember lots of conversations with him, but what stood out, was that he was a true gentleman.

Bill Brookes

This is a story of a remarkable coincidence; Bill Brookes lived in West Court opposite the shop, a lovely old man who liked a tipple at The Bull Hotel in the lunch hour. Bill was rarely seen without his pipe in his mouth. In the days when Bill was a customer, you could still smoke in the shops.

One day in 1988, one of his neighbours, Mary Follett, had brought a pile of old newspapers into the shop. This was a regular occurrence for people to bring in newspapers, as they were used for wrapping bones for dogs etc. Bill came in, as he often did, for some sausages, whilst I was serving him, I noticed he was staring at the pile of newspapers. He was silent and motionless. "What's up Bill?" I said, he pointed to the newspaper headline, which read "Man dies in Portland harbour aged 25" it was April 28th 1965. Bill said "that was my son." "Oh my God," I said. "I'm so sorry," but what was the chance of that? The newspaper just happened to be on the top of the pile. It could have been anywhere else and Bill would not have seen it. Bill just happened to come in when the pile of newspapers was there, and it turned out to be his son who had drowned some twenty three years ago. Remarkable, you never forget these strange coincidences.

Bill and Father had a lot in common. They both enjoyed a drink, smoked a pipe and enjoyed many a chat in the shop. I'm glad they got on; sadly Bill died in 1990 and joined his son in Bridport cemetery.

Arthur Lyall

A respected gentleman, a former partner from Milne and Lyall solicitors, he lived in North Chideock and his wife was great friends with my grandmother Queenie Balson, both being in the Operatic Society together.

A good customer, who was fond of his dogs and fed them very well. Arthur was a true gentleman, very smartly dressed. I always remember his quality leather shoes. I remember Arthur bringing in a bottle of quality champagne for us when my son was born That was the sort of man he was. Generous to a fault. He loved his trips to France for the fine cuisine and wine. I attended Arthur's funeral at St Mary's Church which was packed to the rafters, full of fellow businessmen showing their respect for a great man.

Verdi and Audrey Skinner

A very popular couple who reside in Chideock, I well remember the day Audrey came into our Chideock shop after she had tied her dog up outside to get her weekly shop. Audrey starting talking to another customer whilst I was serving her, she paid for her goods and returned home, forgetting something. Yes. The dog. I phoned Audrey up, have you forgotten something? "No, I don't think so," she replied, "It's got four legs and barks," I said". Audrey was back in a flash and it's something we like to remind her of now and again.

Verdi and Audrey have been two of my favourite customers over the years; you can always have a joke with them. They appreciate good meat and a personal service, and we thank them for their loyalty.

Michael Ebdon

Michael Ebdon, known as the Mayor of Puncknowle, what a character. A Dorset man born and bred, with a fantastic Dorset accent "ooh arr" and it's sometimes hard to understand what he has said. He likes a pint or two or three or more and is often seen walking the lanes of Puncknowle and Swyre with his customary stick in hand.

He used to work for the Dorset Council, was never happier than when out laying hedges, cutting embankments or clearing drains the old fashioned way. Lots of this old manual work has been replaced by murderous machines, which come along and hack the hedge rows to death. There is nothing better than seeing a hedge row laid properly by hand, no machine can do that. Michael was always happy with a hook or spade in his hand. He did a fantastic job in the days when manual workers were valued.

Michael has been a customer of ours for more than fifty years. I recall him asking for beef sausages, then proceeding to eat one raw in the shop. If there were other customers present, they would look at him with dismay and you imagine them thinking, 'they are all a bit strange down here'. He always enjoyed a laugh with my Father and this continues to the present day.

Kathleen Tingay

One morning in March 2013 a lady came into the shop walking with the aid of a Zimmer frame. She approached the counter and asked for two sausages, two slices of bacon and a small piece of black pudding. I served her in my customary way and she paid for the goods and proceeded out the door and into a car driven by her son. My wife Allison knew the lady and she said to me, "how old do you think that lady was?" Now, I think I'm pretty good at guessing people's ages. I thought for a while, summed up the situation and said I reckoned she was about ninety. "You are not right this time," Allison said, "the lady is 105 years old." Good God, I said.

When you think about it, she to date is the oldest person ever to come into our shop. I find this to be an amazing statistic and a great talking point. Just the other day I was talking at the Town Hall, about the business and mentioned this fact and I challenged the audience that maybe one of them could make 106 years old and come into the shop for a free pound of sausages. I'm known for my generosity!

Mrs Tingay attributed her long life to a healthy diet, sherry and a love of music.

The General Public

Dealing with the general public on a daily basis is something that I love and every day brings a new challenge. 99.9% of my customers are a pleasure to serve; the others at times can be hard work. Everyone is different; some people are easy to talk to on any subject imaginable. They are my favourites, it's great to show an interest and be friendly, it's all part of the personal service. Father used to say avoid politics and religion. Most of my male customers have an opinion on sport, this is a good ice breaker, asking which football or rugby or cricket team they support, it's usually the team of their birthplace. Some customers want to engage in conversation, others wish to say very little. I guess it all comes down to confidence. Some customers bring their own bags, unlike customers of years ago, when women shopped with a basket; others expect you to give them a bag every time, that's no problem.

Now the government is trying to minimize the use of plastic bags by charging for them, this may see a return of the hessian bag and wicker basket. We have a recycling problem, because much too much food is packaged sold in plastic wrappers and cartons just to make it look nice, but do we really need it.? It is difficult with fresh meat, because it has to be wrapped well enough not to leak, and plastic bags sometimes are the easy solution.

◆ ◆ ◆ ◆ ◆ ◆

CHAPTER 13

DEATH IN THE FAMILY

Father was pretty active in the shop up until his 80th birthday. He was now spending more time at home, although he was only 150 yards or a phone call away. As he got older he lost his patience and would get very annoyed at some of the questions customers would ask. He became frustrated that he couldn't do what he used to, simple jobs like setting the fire became quite a task. He was still doing all the banking, bookwork and VAT at this time, which was a God-send, and when I eventually took over from him I realized just how much there was to do. Nowadays most of this is completed online, fortunately my wife Allison does most of it. I find I do not have the patience on the computer, and there are times it does not respond, which makes me want to throw it out the window. The internet is a fantastic tool for information and learning, but like everything else, it's fine when it working. With more and more work being submitted online, you almost have to have a full time P.A. My son Billy has spent a lot of time, energy and money on the R J Balson & Son website (www.rjbalson.co.uk) which is proving to be a great asset. Customers can obtain our contact details and personally call the shop to place an order. There are some lovely old photos on the website as well as the history of the business and you can watch our BBC documentary and view current awards we have received. We are now involved with social networking on Facebook and Twitter, which also helps with our advertising and of course keeps us updated with the latest news and gossip.

Father was now spending more time in his greenhouse, which he dearly loved. He was great at growing orchids and freesias. He would sometimes bring a good specimen to display in the shop. I was amazed how many customers would comment on them. Stoke Lodge always has a good display of flowers.

Father was gradually slowing down. Well what do you expect? He was now 87 years old. He was never a person to complain or visit the doctor, but things had changed. He wasn't feeling himself and had a few funny turns, as he put it. We were very concerned, and as he was reluctant to go to the doctors, I persuaded his G.P., Dr Skellern, to call in for a home visit and check him out. After a couple of visits to the hospital and a series of tests, father was diagnosed with a large tumour on his lung which was inoperable. He inevitably went downhill very slowly but very courageously. He knew what was happening but didn't want to trouble anyone.

One moment, which will remain with me forever, was when I went into the kitchen to see him. He was sat at the end of table in his usual seat in front of the Aga. He had tears in this eyes. I said "are you in pain dad?", no he replied "what's up then I asked?" ''I want to say goodbye but don't know how to." Well that started me off, and we sat there holding each other and crying our eyes out. We are all human and we all have feelings, and I loved my dad. He knew the end was near. He hated hospitals and wanted to die at home, just like his mother and Auntie May before him, and he did just that. On Saturday 23rd July 2011 at 5pm, just after the shop had closed, Father peacefully passed away with all the family around the bed. He was on morphine for the pain and we toasted his life with a glass of sherry.

I'm welling up now just writing this as it is still painful; Father got his last wish, dying at home. It was a credit to Mum and the family for nursing him. We all took it in turns to help with the nursing, with the help of the Marie Curie nurses, who do such wonderful jobs. I think it's the sort of death anyone would want, dignified and deserved. If I could choose how do die, then I would like to die just like Father did, surrounded by people that love you, in your own bed in your own home, but I'm not looking forward to it.

Mum was now living in Stoke Lodge by herself, so Jane, Rudie and family moved in to keep an eye on her. She is doing very well, although she has limited mobility. Her body is worn out from all that dancing on the stage and she is now 88, but in good spirits.

The Funeral

Monday 8th August 2011 at St. John the Baptist Church Symondsbury, I wasn't sure how many people would be there. After all, he had outlived most of his friends, but the church was packed with customers, friends and family. Reverend Janis Moore did us proud. A lovely service. It meant so much more as the Reverend is a family friend, who had known Father all her life. My brother Mike and I gave tributes. I can get up in front of a crowd and speak no problem, but this was a little different. A tribute to your own father with the family weeping around you, was not easy. This was probably the hardest thing I have ever done. Trying to keep it all together and not break down, but I did and did him proud. I had to. It's the last thing you can do for someone; even got a few laughs along the way.

Then on to Bridport cemetery where father was buried next to Queenie, his mum and Pop, his dad, in the family plot. We returned to Symondsbury where a reception was held at The Ilchester Arms with lovely people reminiscing with stories about Father. It was particularly nice that two of Mike's former professional footballing friends from his Exeter days, travelled up to pay their respects. Jimmy Giles and John Wingate had become good family friends over the years and it was so nice to see them there. My son Billy was going to give his tribute to his granddad at the funeral, but he was unable to attend as his wife Olivia was in hospital giving birth to a daughter Esme, a sister for Freddie. It's strange that as one dies another is born.

There were many lovely tributes to Father in the local press, and we have lots of photos of him in the shop. He is always with us. Gone but not forgotten. This was another reason for writing this book, so future generations could read and learn about his life. For some unknown reason, I felt compelled to write a poem about my Father. Don't ask me why. I'm not poetic. I have never attempted to write before, but I must admit I found it quite easy to get the words to rhyme, and within half an hour I came up with the following, which I entered into a poetry competition and it was published in a poetry book.

I actually found writing the poem very therapeutic, and I think putting one's memories down on paper helped to ease the pain of losing a loved one. One of the true stories I told at Father's funeral in my tribute to him, and which made the congregation chuckle, was that Father always walked to the shop at 6.30 in the morning, leaving Stoke Lodge some 150 yards away. He always walked in the middle of the road (as long as there was no traffic). One of our customers an early riser across the road in West Court flats, had for some time watched Father walking in the middle of the road to the shop. One day her curiosity got the better of her, and she came into the shop and asked, "Mr Balson, why do you always walk down the middle of the road in the morning?" Father replied "because all the dog shit is on the pavement." There was a method in his madness!

◆ ◆ ◆ ◆ ◆ ◆

DAD

Dads are so very special
You only get the one
You must respect and love them
Even when their time is done

Their guidance and their wisdom
They teach you to be true
Be thankful for the knowledge
That they pass on to you

Remember all the good times
You spent with your dad
Don't let all those memories
Make you feel sad

The jokes and all the laughter
And all those playful pranks
For all those lovely memories
We give you dad our thanks

England's oldest family Butcher
Not many a man can say
Dad's played his part in history
Up to the present day

But now dad's gone and left us
A big hole left behind
But we will never forget you dad
You're always on our mind

He is looking down from heaven
Guiding us now, from above
Inspiring us to carry on
He's the dad that we all love.

CHAPTER 14

HEALTHY EATING, RECIPES AND AWARDS

People are living longer now than ever before, life expectancy is around 80 years, whereas in the 1950s it was only about 50. A better diet, better knowledge of medicine, and improved living conditions have all contributed to this. The newspapers are experts at scaremongering, stating that certain foods are bad for you. One week it's red meat, the next it's coffee, the next it's sugar, I firmly believe that a well-balanced diet of meat/fish and two veg, is the healthiest. I would love to do a survey on the average age of butchers living in this country, you would have thought that most butchers would eat more meat than the average person; I know my family have done. They have all reached a good age before leaving this earth, anything in moderation is good for you, and a bit of what you fancy does you good. Certain foods have become healthier over the years. Let's take sausages for example, years ago they contained a lot more fat than they do now. Sausages are now a very healthy and nutritious meal, with so many different varieties available. They can be cooked in almost any way to make them one of the most versatile foods of today.

Our best selling traditional pork breakfast sausage has been made using our own secret family recipe for over 100 years but now with a much leaner meat content. The sausage has been a family favourite for many years, and also my personal favourite. Bangers and mash is great pub grub, and you will find it on all good pub menus. All sausages for sale in our shop are very low in fat, just cook them and see what comes out, nothing is the answer. In the old days when sausages had a lot of fat in them, they would explode when cooking that's why there were called Bangers. The kangaroo/ostrich sausages contain no fat at all and are zero rated for cholesterol. Our newest sausage the free-range chicken sausage is proving very popular with everyone, especially those who can't eat pork, whether for religious or allergy reasons. The chicken sausage is a must for the non-red meat connoisseurs. We stock a range of over twenty varieties, which are regularly available in the shop.

Our sausage making was made much easier when we purchased a new automatic machine, which has the capacity to hold 60lb of sausage meat. This has improved production immensely compared to the old fashioned machine where you had to turn the handle. Each week we make between 500-1,000 lb of sausages. I'm often asked what my favourite meat is. This is a very tough question for a man who loves it all. I think I would say a mixed grill, as this is an assortment of different meats: steak, chop, gammon, sausage, liver and kidney, what a combination! What would be better? Don't forget the chips, onion rings, peas and a couple of eggs.

I have always been a quantity man. When I say that, I mean I want to have a meal and be full up. There is nothing worse than paying a lot of money for a little portion of fancy food, which has been artistically arranged on a plate three times the size of the food on it. Some of the Master Chef cookery competitions seem to be a contest about presentation and artistic impression, rather than producing a good meal that is going to fill you up.

FAGGOTS

Gran taught me how to make faggots at an early age. They are a combination of pork, liver, sage, onion and potato, but of course our recipe is secret. Although now made in much larger batches than when Gran was making them, the ingredients and taste are the same.

In the war years when food was short, butchers would put anything they could find in faggots, but those days are long gone. Faggots are great value and so easy to prepare for a meal, as they are already cooked they only have to be heated.

Here is my recipe, take four faggots. Put them into a saucepan. Add a handful of peas, frozen, tinned, mushy or garden or whatever you fancy. Add one sliced onion, top up with gravy and heat through over medium heat until piping hot. Serve with chips or mash. A good healthy meal in ten minutes, who says cooking is difficult?!

Another of my favourite recipes, which again is quick and easy, is pan fried pheasant breast. The pheasant breast is a good healthy nutritious and economical meal. Take four breasts, boned and skinned, and heat a little olive oil in a pan with chopped shallots/onions and mushrooms. When reduced, fry the pheasant breasts for two minutes either side. Serve with rice or new potatoes. Quick and easy and very healthy and don't forget the red wine.

AWARDS

I'm proud to say that our sausages and bacon have won many awards over

Bridport Food Festival 2014
R J Balson & Son, proud winners of the Liz Field award for the Best Dressed Stall
Allison and Jane receiving the award

the recent years. All our sausages have won gold at some time or another, at the B.P.E.X Awards and at the Taste of the West Awards.

Our dry cure bacon was voted overall champion at the Taste of the West 2012. All our bacon is cured from local free range pork from Childhay Manor. My step-daughter Steph is head of our bacon department, and does a great job selecting the best loins to be cured.

Our beef and horseradish sausages won the South West of England Championship in 2010/2011. We were finalists in the Dorset Food and Drink awards in 2011. We have also been finalists in the Dorset Business Awards Family Business Section in 2012 and 2013. We won the Best Dressed Stall at the Bridport Food Festival in 2014 and to top it off we were voted Retail Family Business of the Year winners at an award ceremony in London in June 2014.

It is important to enter product awards; it keeps us on the ball and helps us stay ahead of the competition. They are usually held annually, and can come at a cost i.e. entry fees and postage, but winning gold awards makes it well worth it, and reassures us and our customers that we are up there producing the best food available. At the same time it is also great to meet other producers.

◆ ◆ ◆ ◆ ◆ ◆

Richard & Allison Balson
Retail Family Business Award 2014

R.DURTNELL & SONS LIMITED
BUILDING CONTRACTORS

JAD/PAB   21 November 2011

R J Balson & Son Inc
9 West Allington
Bridport
Dorset
DT6 5BJ

Dear Sirs

Congratulations on your splendid publicity both on the radio and in the newspapers and I am writing to you to enquire whether you would be interested in becoming a Tercentenarian.

Let me explain.

The Tercentenarians Club was formed 40 odd years ago, and is a collection of family businesses that have been trading for more than 300 years. It all started in 1967 when Richard Early of Richard Early Blanket Maker of Whitney put a letter in the Times saying it was his firm's 300th birthday and if anybody could match it he would buy them lunch! My father, along with some other gentlemen, responded and they all had a fine time visiting Oxford. My father then invited the group to come to Kent the following year and that they should bring their wives. This they did; again had a pleasant day, and decided to form the Club to perpetuate the idea.

I should say at the outset that we are a Club that has no written rules, no subscriptions or great formality, we rather jog along by consent and membership is by invitation only. As the years have gone by we have amended the unwritten rules (if/is that possible?!) because our numbers were getting rather thin.

In reality what this means is that once a year one of the members, and we generally do this by informal rotation, hosts a day for all others to come to his place of business. We gather in the morning, have a pleasant so called Annual General Meeting followed by lunch and perhaps a tour of the host's works or a visit to an interesting nearby attraction. The pattern for the day is entirely down to each host who foots the bill for that day!

If the notion appeals to you, I would be delighted to discuss matters with you, but at this juncture you may care to know that next year's Tercentenarian meeting is on Thursday 17 May 2012 and the host for the day will be Fortnum & Mason from Piccadilly. Last year we hosted the day and we held it at the Turner Contemporary in Margate, a new gallery that we had recently constructed.

R. Durtnell & Sons Ltd. Rectory Lane, Brasted, Westerham, Kent TN16 1JR
Telephone 01959 564105 Fax 01959 564756 E-mail rds@durtnell.co.uk www.durtnell.co.uk
Regional Office: The Governor's House, 101 Alexandra Road, Farnborough, Hants GU14 6BN

CHAPTER 15

THE TERCENTENARIAN CLUB

In November 2011 out of the blue I received a letter asking if R J Balson & Son would like to join the Tercentenarians, 'what and who are the Tercentenarians?' I thought. I read the letter and the invite to join did appeal to us. We accepted the invitation and went to our first meeting at Fortnum and Mason, London in the newly refurbished Queen's Jubilee Tea Room in May 2012. It was a splendid, overwhelming occasion where we met all the other members of the club in fantastic surroundings. We were given an exclusive tour of the store and then down to the wine cellar, where we toasted with champagne and finally an exquisite three course lunch.

We are very proud to be members of this exclusive club. After travelling to Huddersfield to John Brooke and Son Holdings Ltd in 2013 for their annual meeting. It was now our turn to host the event. So, on the 19th May the exclusive Tercentenarian Club came to Bridport for the very first time. We met at The Avenue Restaurant for lunch, then everyone took to the floor for 10 minutes to describe their past year in business, good, bad or indifferent. Then it was down to the shop at West Allington where I gave a brief history talk about the business and Rudie, our head sausage maker, gave a sausage making demonstration. This enthralled and entertained the thirty-two strong audience, before a couple of the group, Alex Durtnell and Simon Hoare tried their hand at sausage making. This really was entertaining, sausages of all different shapes and sizes!

We had a great day, enjoyed by all members, but what I found most pleasing was that only one of the thirty-two present had visited Bridport before. They all commented on what a lovely town Bridport was and how lucky we are to live here. Well, we know that. I have been touched by the lovely emails and hand written letters of gratitude from the members for the marvellous day. We look forward to the annual meetings as we have made new friends from different walks of life, from all over the country.

Current Members of the Tercentenarian Club

R J Balson & Son, Berry Bros., John Brooke & Son, C Hoare & Co.,
R Durtnell & Son Ltd., Peter Freebody, Folkes Holdings,
Fortnum & Mason, James Lock & Co., Shepherd Neame,
Toye Kenning & Spencer, Whitechapel Bell Foundry.

◆ ◆ ◆ ◆ ◆ ◆

Tercentenarian Meeting 2014   Joan Balson and family, and members of the Tercentenarian Club.
Photo courtesy of Stuart Broom – View from Newspapers.

CHAPTER 16

TYING THE KNOT AND GOOD FRIENDS

We got married on 1st June 2012. The reception was held in a marquee in the garden of our home in Symondsbury, with eighty guests to celebrate the occasion and with a blessing from the Rev Janice Moore.

It was a wonderful day. Our families rallied round to help with the catering and organising, and yes we ran out of beer. We wished Father could have been there with us, but he was in our thoughts.

My best man was David (Diddle) Warren. Now, Dave is a very popular man. He told me he had been the Best Man on six previous occasions, but what he forgot to tell me, was only one of the couples was still married.

Dave is one of the best, will always do you a favour, and help you out if he can. I have played a lot of sport with Dave. He always gives 100% and is a tough competitor. Dave gave a great best man speech and had everyone in fits of laughter.

Richard and Allison Balson Wedding June 2012

Richard and best man David (Diddle) Warren

Whilst talking about Dave, I must mention another friend Paul Evans. Well Dave, Paul and I entered into a "Come Dine with me" challenge. The challenge was just for the men, with the wives coming along to score, but not cook. We had three very good evenings, followed by entertainment. I, being the butcher and having a good knowledge of meat and cookery, was obviously the favourite to win, and I did. We had such fun along the way, plenty of mickey taking and jokes etc…

Due to the success of this competition we decided to have another the following year. Somehow Dave and Paul colluded and fixed the scoring, enabling them to come joint first and me second or in their words LAST… Dave and Paul have taken great pleasure in this and constantly remind me that I finished last. I have had to have counselling (only joking) to help me come to terms with losing my title in such a mischievous way. Paul made a mistake adding up the scores. Now when I went to school 9+9+9+9 equalled 36. Alas, poor Paul who didn't have the benefit of a Sir John Colfox School education totalled my score at 26. Now, I'm not saying Paul cheated, but let's just say that what he lacks in height, he more than makes up for in craftiness, but I do love the man.

◆◆◆◆◆◆

CHAPTER 17

WINDOW ADVERTISING

We like to advertise our products on our shop window. White face paint does the trick, shows up and does not wash off in the rain. Father would mark up special offers in big writing, so passing cars could observe.

On April Fool's Day he liked to put a joke up on the window, 'elephant and cucumber sausages' comes to mind or 'faggot roller required, apply within'. It always brought a smile to customers' faces. I well remember the day when I made a slight mistake in my spelling. I was sent out to mark up pork tenderloins on the window. I inadvertently put the 'i' and the 'o' round the wrong way, which spelt 'tenderlions', and customers came in to enquire how much the lion meat was. Took a while to get over that one.

When the BBC correspondent John Sergeant was on Strictly Come Dancing, and he was getting through on the sympathy of the public vote, rather than on his ability, we wrote on the window, 'Vote John Sergeant' for a bit of fun. Little did I know that I would meet the man a year later when he came into the shop to film 'The One Show'. I found him to be a wonderful man. It's amazing to think he has interviewed all the famous people in the world, politicians, and world leaders, when working as political journalist of the BBC. He has been on the spot at most of the news stories of the last 30 years and was one of the few white reporters standing in front of the Lincoln memorial in Washington DC when American civil rights leader Martin Luther King gave his famous, 'I have a dream' speech in 1963. 50 years on, he is interviewing me, England's oldest family butcher, unbelievable. I found John easy to talk to, although he seemed reluctant to discuss his time on 'Strictly' amongst the beautiful dancers with spray tans on the show.

I found John easy to work with and he was glad to purchase some meat to take back home to London. Now, as you know, John is a big 'hat man' so I pointed him in the direction of Roger Snook's hat shop in West Street, where I believe he purchased a few hats. Mr Snook's shop has the most fantastic display of different hats of all shapes and sizes you will ever see. Roger is a credit to Bridport and another old established business trading since 1896.

John Sergeant was a great conversationalist, happy to talk about an old

Richard Balson and John Sergeant February 2013

customer of mine, Sir Robin Day, who was also a political correspondent for many years. During his retirement he lived at St Mary's Cottage, Morcombelake, Bridport with his wife and sons. I have fond memories of talking to Sir Robin, when he would shop at our Chideock shop in the 1980s. He was a dogmatic character who had given many a politician a good grilling. When shopping with us, he was almost in disguise in a large woollen duffle coat and walking boots, unlike his appearance on television when he was well suited with his customary large bow tie. Happy memories.

◆ ◆ ◆ ◆ ◆ ◆

SIR ROBIN DAY, 16 NORTH COURT, GREAT PETER STREET, SW1P 3LL
01-222 1330

Many thanks The pheasant was excellent as was the filley! RD.

St Mary's Cottage, Morcombelake

16 NORTH COURT,
GREAT PETER STREET,
LONDON, SW1P 3LL
01- 222 1330

Balsons
Butchers
Chideoc

Aug 16

Enclosed with thanks my
Cheque for your recent delivery
of steak etc. (It was excellent).

If possible, please could you deliver
another fillet and some mushrooms
at my cottage on Tuesday Sept 2nd?
I'd be grateful if you could do this
but if it is not convenient I shall
quite understand.
(Please leave it in the washroom —
which is open — on the right of
the entrance.)

Thanks

R Day

Letter received by R J Balson & Son from Robin Day

CHAPTER 18

YEARLY CALENDAR OF EVENTS

Throughout the year each month has a different level of trade. For many reasons the weather, holiday periods and the economic climate. Busy times and quiet times make up the year.

January

A relatively quiet month after the New Year celebrations. It's good to have a slight rest after the Christmas rush. However, during this time, it is nice to have more time to be able to chat with your customers and get to know new customers better. Our television documentary is aired and the response has been overwhelming.

Burns Night is celebrated on the 25th January with most pubs and restaurants buying our finest award winning Macsween's haggis for their parties. The trade in January is usually like the weather at this time of year. Gloomy.

February

The first of February brings another shooting season to an end. This is a good time to buy the cock bird pheasants, which are rounded up by the keepers, whilst the hen birds are left for breeding. It's a time to catch up on all the odd jobs, which have accumulated through the year: some painting, repairs and minor jobs, which are always required on an old building such as ours. The outside of the shop is painted every other year. Valentine's Day sees an influx of men buying steak for their sweethearts, in an attempt to cook a romantic meal for the special occasion.

A good time for staff to take a short break, before we start to get really busy.

March

Spring is upon us. Early new season's lamb is young, sweet and tender, and now at its best. The local campsites begin to open. Familiar faces begin to reappear, arriving to spring clean their caravans.

Mothering Sunday is a day to celebrate with the family and a good joint of beef with the ones you love. March 17th is St Patrick's Day. Beef and Guinness sausages are very popular, not just in the U.K but also in America where vast numbers of the Irish have emigrated and are buying Balson's sausages in Costco around the country.

Seaside restaurants begin to reopen for the season, and National Butcher's Week is upon us at the end of the month.

April

Easter holidays are upon us. Pubs, hotels and restaurants begin to see an increase in trade. The level of trade depends on the weather.

In the shop, it's faggots, faggots and more faggots. Since our television documentary in January 2014, faggot sales have tripled. Even The Seasider fish and chip restaurant at West Bay has them on their menu.

St George's Day on the 23rd April. A national feast day to celebrate his life and death in AD 303, just slightly older than The Balsons.

May

Traditional English May Day celebrations include Morris dancing, crowning a May Queen and dancing around a Maypole. Sausage production increases with the extra volume of customers arriving in Bridport. Two Bank Holidays bring extra trade to our market town. B & Bs now fully booked, offering our sausages and bacon in abundance. Customers still mentioning our documentary being repeated throughout the year.

June

Shop volume is increasing due to summer footfall. Rudie is tied to the sausage machine for long periods of the day. Sausages, kebabs and burgers all selling well. It's time for the local food festival, which is great for PR as well as trade. Bridport has a great reputation for local food and excellent food producers.

The food festival is a good opportunity for us to mix with other local producers in a lovely atmosphere, just one mile from our shop. It is very well organized and after ten years the committee has it down to a T. A great social occasion attracting visitors from all over the South West.

Trading at a different venue gives our more attractive staff an opportunity to man the stall. Allison, Jane and her daughter Tilly do a great job selling sausages and bacon, cooking samples for customers to taste. I'm always amazed at how many people come to our stall and ask, 'where is your shop in Bridport?' Well, if they have only just moved into the town or are a visitor, then the question is acceptable, but for people who have lived in Bridport for 10 years or more? You just assume that having been in our present shop since 1892, everyone knows where your shop is, but this is not always the case.

July

The children break up from school. Families arrive for their holidays and this is the beginning of the busy six week period. It's nice to welcome back familiar faces here on holiday, unbelievable that yet another year has passed since they were last in the shop. We take delivery of our first 250 special edition R J Balson ceramic mugs to commemorate our 500 years in business, now on sale in the shop.

August

August is a very busy month for everyone. Carnivals and fetes are in full swing. The grouse season starts on the 12th August known as the 'glorious 12th'. The Melplash Agricultural Show which attracts thousands of visitors each year is always held on the Thursday before the August Bank Holiday, with records showing the first society show was held in 1847.

I was privileged to be asked last year to judge the inaugural Melplash Show sausage competition. I was told there would be about six entries. Well, to my amazement there were about eighteen. Pretty good for the first time this category had been held.

I enjoyed tasting the sausages, especially as it was being filmed by the BBC for my documentary. Sadly it wasn't shown in the programme, which was a shame because they had some great footage. In the past Father went to the show on many occasions to judge the lambs. Here he is with the late Jack Norman.

The third week in August sees the arrival of the Symondsbury Flower Show at the Ilchester Arms, where local villagers battle it to out to be recognised as having the best vegetables and flowers in the area. At the end of the day I have great pleasure auctioning the produce for a worthy cause.

August Bank Holiday arrives which is our second busiest week of the year apart from Christmas. On the Sunday of that weekend the Symene Sports Club

Melplash Show 1994 Jack Norman and Donald Balson

Fete, which I have helped organise for the past 28 years, takes place. We are grateful for the Bank Holiday Monday off, to recuperate.

September

The 1st of September sees the start of the season for partridge shooting. Children return to school and relieved parents can't believe they have survived the six weeks of school holidays.

The retired generation flock to Dorset for peace and quiet and a stroll along the Jurassic coast.

The hat festival attracts visitors wearing hats of all shapes and sizes from all over the world. A great social gathering with everyone jovial and happy regardless of what they are wearing.

I wear a hat every day at work, the famous straw boater was popular as casual summer headgear in the late 19th century and early 20th century, especially for boating or sailing, hence the name. They were supposedly worn by FBI agents as a sort of unofficial uniform in the pre-war years.

October

After a hectic Summer season, October is a much quieter month. However, there is lots of interesting game available.

The shooting season starts on the 1st of the month, plenty of pheasants, pigeons, mallard, rabbits now in season. This is the month that we make our annual onion run from Plymouth to Roscoff. Rudie takes the ferry over night and arrives in Roscoff early the next morning. He arrives at his destination, just a couple of miles from the port. On reaching Paul Caroff's House, his cargo awaits in a nearby barn. Over 100 strings of award winning french onions, garlic and shallots, the top produce from the Roscoff Onion Festival which takes place in the last week of August. Balson's van is full to the brim. In fact, next year we must get a bigger vehicle as we could sell double what we are able to bring back.

Our local regular customers place their orders for the onions every year. This tradition has been taking place for over 40 years. When Paul Caroff first started coming to England to sell his onions, he used to rent a storage container in the Poole Docks, sit down at night and string the onions, which is an art in itself. The next day he would venture out on his bicycle to sell them. After about thirty years, he had built up quite a customer base. Like all Johnny Onion men, he started with his bicycle and progressed to a van and then a car and trailer. He enjoyed his trips to England and over the years built up special relationships and made good friends with many of his customers. Paul liked a glass of quality red wine or two or three. Father never paid Paul for his onions but instead would barter, and Paul would take home the finest Dorset lamb in exchange.

French onions are very strong and have a pink bloom to them. I love them for supper with a little Dorset Blue Vinney. The only trouble is you can still taste them the next morning.

In the year 2000, Paul's health started to deteriorate, and his doctor refused to allow him to travel overseas. Paul said, "if you want the onions you better come and get them." So, that was the start of our annual trips to Roscoff. The first year Rudie and Father went over. Obviously, it was a great advantage having Rudie the Frenchman on board with the language and trying to explain at customs why an English butcher's van was full to the brim with French onions.

Our customers love the French onions, and it really is a wonderful sight when they are hung all around the shop. A fantastic display and the smell is wonderful. Then, just one week later they are all gone. Sold. There is something special about hanging up a string of onions in the kitchen or larder. They look good, they taste good and are so easy to use.

French Onions arrive at Balsons the Butchers

Sadly, Paul passed away a few years ago. He was a colourful character who became good friends with my father. They really looked forward to seeing each other and doing business together.

Paul's wife Marie and their sons are carrying on the onion business in Roscoff and we look forward to our next trip. Rudie in particular, enjoys returning to his native country, even if it is only for 24 hours. Sometimes doing something different seems like a welcome change.

November

The colder weather is with us, which makes our job much easier. The pheasants are getting bigger and the local fresh venison is at its best. I recall my father being very good friends with Alan Fooks from Poorton. The Fooks are a great farming family renowned for their Dorset Horn lambs. Alan would phone up, "want a Deer Don?" He would bring one or two to the shop in his pick-up. Alan was a lovely man.

Father showed me how to skin a deer at an early age. We would hang them up in the old slaughter room at the back of the shop. This room is also known as the "salt house" because all the pickling and brining was completed in this room, before the days of refrigeration. Father had a special skinning knife with a curved blade, to make the job easier. Once skinned it was into the fridge to set and hang for a couple of days.

The Dorset Chamber of Trade, host their Business Awards Gala Dinner. It's a pleasure to be involved, and great to be recognised as one of the best. The 30th November is St Andrew's Day. Haggis time again. Christmas is just a month away. Scary!

December

Christmas is such a busy time for butchers. The most important time as families gather around the table for a traditional meal to celebrate Christmas and the birth of Christ. Butchers work extra-long hours at Christmas and by the time Christmas Day comes, it's a good meal, a couple of drinks and a sleep for the rest of the day.

This is followed by two to three days of holiday for us. Most firms close down for a week or two during this time. That's very nice but in our trade it's impossible as you have to keep turning the stock over. The maximum number of days off is only four. Anyway, by that time I'm bored and ready to get back to work, and look forward to the new year. More and more customers every year are buying boneless turkey breast, as opposed to the traditional whole bird on the bone. It is all about convenience and the carcass is not required any more.

Our Christmas hampers have been very successful and contain a selection of festive treats such as turkey, gammon, pork, beef, sausage meat and pigs in blankets. Everything you need for a tasty Christmas lunch. Also very popular is our three bird roast, which can be any combination of birds rolled into one.

The pubs and hotels are all busy with their Christmas parties and work dinners. Christmas is a busy time for everyone, and for us butchers, it can be quite stressful.

The Symondsbury Mummers perform their traditional pagan play around the town which brings laughter and merriment to the audience. If you have never seen the Mummers in action, it's a must .

Memories of Father going down to West Bay for his annual Christmas Day swim come flooding back.

Free-range turkeys for the Christmas table

CHAPTER 19

TELEVISION DOCUMENTARY

In early 2013 the BBC approached me about making a documentary about England's Oldest Family Business. After much discussion with the family, we agreed.

During the summer of 2013 we were invaded by film crews. I found this to be an exciting and pleasurable experience. It was a hot summer that year, and the sun was always shining during filming. The shots of Bridport high street looked fantastic accompanied by the seasonal carnival bunting which adorned the streets. It was hoped it would be a great advert not just for us, but for the whole of Bridport. Twenty four hours of filming had to be condensed into a one hour programme. So, sadly a lot of the footage was left on the 'cutting room' floor.

The programme was called 'Hidden Histories' and was aired on BBC4 on January 15th 2014 and we were the first in a series of three programmes. It was a fantastic advert for R J Balson & Son and the programme has been repeated several times already, so this helps to keep the ball rolling, so to speak. The response from the documentary has been unbelievable: emails, letters, and phone calls from all over the world. One of my favourite stories was from a man called Ted Ward, who went on to tell me that he was born and bred in Bridport. His parents owned and ran Bannister House, an electrical store that was situated next to the Palace cinema. In 1950, when he left school, his first job, was working in Balson's, cleaning the tripe and delivering on the trade bicycle. He went on to reminisce about delivering to the West Mead Hotel (which was Bridport's top hotel situated in West Allington). As he approached the entrance to the hotel, two big dogs would come bounding down the drive ready to attack him. This always stuck in Ted's mind. I don't think it was a pleasurable memory but it was so nice of Ted to take the time to write to me, as he is in his 80s and lives near Guildford in Surrey. It is so nice to hear about stories from before I was born.

The documentary taught me a lot about my family and the journey they had taken since 1515. Prior to that, I only knew about our family from around 1890 when we moved into our current shop. Once you move on in time a couple of generations, it is all forgotten about.

This is one of the reasons I felt duty bound to write these memories of my time in the business. After all, I look upon myself as the current custodian at the helm at this particular time. Hopefully, it will be a record for future generations to read and keep, and make them think.

Poor Arthur Balson, who had his head blown off by a shot gun in 1859 and poor Robert John Balson, who took his own life by cutting his throat in 1930. 'How did this make you feel?' I was asked by the producer. Well, what do you expect in a period of history spanning 500 years? It's not all going to be good news. Both Arthur and Robert John had played their part in the family history, and in this book their memories will live on for future generations to read about, and hopefully respect their input on this family business.

Arthur's death was a tragic accident, which poor 10 year old Tom was burdened with for the rest of his life. It was a tribute to Arthur that his funeral took place on a Sunday, so all the traders and towns people could attend. I have not known a funeral to take place on a Sunday before.

As for Robert John, he had retired, done his time, and maybe become depressed. Who knows? But, if you were in a psychiatric hospital in those days the only treatment you would receive was shock treatment. Poor man.

As we know, through the early years the Balson family were also involved in the pub trade in Bridport, with the market shambles only trading on a Wednesday and Saturday. A lot of pubs had small slaughtering rooms in the out buildings. Going into the pub trade meant they could sell beer over the bar and meat out the back door seven days a week, before the introduction of the high street shops.

Obviously the most important fact to come out of the documentary, was when they discovered that we were 20 years older than what we had thought. 499 years seems a good time to write this book and share our history as we approach our 500 years in business. In making the documentary, Producer Chis Durlacher and Assistant Producer Tom Swingler were very easy to work with and became like family. A day on location in the historical town of York, visiting the old shambles was a real treat. York is a hub of the railway network and confectionery manufacturing centre and steeped with history. We would have liked to have spent more time there, going around the museums and walking the city walls which were built in 71 AD (so I guess we have a while to catch them up!).

Our visit to York was rounded off with a meal courtesy of the BBC in The Guy Fawkes Inn which stands in the shadow of York Minister. Apparently, he was born there in 1570, before trying to blow up the Houses of Parliament.

The Shambles York

The Shambles is Europe's best preserved medieval street and was once crammed with butchers' shops. These days you're more likely to get an ice cream and post card than a pound of mince.

◆ ◆ ◆ ◆ ◆ ◆

CHAPTER 20

ALBERT BALSON AND JAMES COLSTON HILL

Albert Balson and James Colston Hill were two relatives I felt I had to include in this book for their bravery. They were not butchers. They chose a different path in life, but they certainly deserve a mention in different ways.

Chief Petty Officer Albert Balson BEM, DSM, RN

Albert was born on the 12th February 1885 in Allington parish. He was a Balson who chose a different career to being a butcher. At school he was an unenthusiastic scholar and often skipped school to help a local farmer. When the local school attendance officer found out where he had bunked off to, Albert set the farmer's dog on him.

Notwithstanding his affinity with the soil, Albert wanted to be a sailor, and as a boy he walked to Portland to enlist in the Royal Navy. He was taken into boy service on the 2nd October 1900, four months before his 14th birthday, signing on for 12 years' service. By 1911 he was a leading seaman on HMS Powerful. Then, on 6th December, he transferred to the Terra Nova at Lyttleton for service with Captain R F Scott's British National Antarctic Expedition 1910-13.

Whilst on the Terra Nova he took part in her second and third voyage to the Antarctic and, as a consequence of his good service, he received the Polar Medal. On the Expedition's return, Albert went back to the Royal Navy to become a diver, and had an eventful war. In 1917, the White Star Laurentic ran into a minefield, laid by the German submarine U-80, and struck two mines, with deadly consequences. The Laurentic sank in 45 minutes. There was a heavy loss of life. News of the sinking spread, but the public were not informed that the Laurentic had taken 3,211 gold bars with her to the bottom of the sea. Some five million pounds in gold being transported secretly to pay for U.S munitions was now laying twenty-three fathoms off the Irish mainland. The loss was a financial disaster for the British Treasury, so the Admiralty took immediate steps to recover the lost bullion. Lt Commander Damant RN was appointed to lead a small handpicked team of divers including Albert Balson, who was the senior diver, to recover the gold. They quickly found the wreck, but had great difficulty scrambling over her steeply sloping decks. During the first summer they recovered £800,000 worth of gold, but by September the weather had deteriorated and they were forced to close down operations.

Arthur Balson BEM. DSM, RN   Chief Petty Officer

Salvage work continued year on year until 1924, by which time they had accounted for 3,189 of the gold bars. They missed only 22 of them, which are still missing to this day. Commander Damant, who had been invested with the order of the British Empire (OBE) in 1919, was promoted to Captain. The eleven divers, arguably the Royal Navy's best, were each awarded the British Empire Medal and shared a bounty of £6,379.

In 1945 Albert Balson returned to civilian life in his native Dorset. He died on the 18th December 1950 at The Holly Lodge Nursing Home in Parkstone at the age of 65. He had braved the harsh Antarctic under Captain R F Scott and been challenged by the recovery of thousands of bars of gold from the wreck of the Laurentic. A truly incredible life story of a naval serviceman.

James Colston Hill

My great-grandfather on my mother's side, James Colston Hill, was born at 19 Albert Street, Ryde, Isle of Wight. His father is described as an engine fitter. The family then moved to Southampton and were living at 121 Northam Road. James married Annie Elizabeth Stephens in 1873 and later had four children, though one died in infancy: May Irene (b.1893) Isabel Christina (b.1898) and James Norman Colston (b. 1903). The family then moved to 64 Cromwell Road, Southampton where James signed on as first class chief steward on the Titanic. His wage was £3 15 sh per month.

On Sunday 14th April 1912, James was one of the many who perished on that fateful night after the Titanic struck an iceberg. His body was later recovered and numbered 152 by the MacKay/Bennett – the first of four ships chartered by the White Star Line to search for bodies in the aftermath of the sinking.

James was buried at sea on the 24th April that year, which would have been in the vicinity of Nova Scotia, Canada. His body was still suited in his steward's uniform and in his pocket was one pipe, one stud and two ships keys.

◆ ◆ ◆ ◆ ◆ ◆

CHAPTER 21

FATHER'S DAY

It's the 15th June 2014, Father's Day. A lovely sunny day. "Any day is good if you are here to see it, even a dismal dark winter's day", that was one of Father's sayings.

I have just got back from Bridport cemetery somewhat teary eyed. Father's Day is special for everyone. Father was never a lover of flowers on the grave. He always used to say, "bring up a bottle of beer and pour it over the grave." I have done this on a few occasions, but I must admit I had half emptied the bottle first. Today I didn't take flowers or beer, instead I took the first chapter of this book and read to him, Gran and other members of the family surrounding Father for company. I'm sure he would have approved of this book.

Bridport cemetery is a special place, with wonderful views and grand tall trees. A tranquil final resting place, full of special memories for everyone. As I look around the cemetery, I think how lucky we are to live here in Bridport. Green fields, the birds singing and the wonderful smell of the clean Dorset air. I am thankful for good health, surrounded by good people and in a job which I love. Yes it's hard work, but some people thrive on keeping busy and I'm one of them. Never a dull moment. Live life to the full, eat good meat, drink and be merry.

My visit to the cemetery brings all those memories flooding back of working with Father, and Gran sitting on the stool in the office. It's therapeutic and in your mind you are with them again. Then, in the next breath you realise how lucky you are to be breathing the Dorset air. So, I finish reading the first chapter, and leave the cemetery with a tear in my eye, but I feel better for the visit.

Returning home I receive a phone call from my son Billy, wishing me a happy Father's Day. I'm smiling again.

◆ ◆ ◆ ◆ ◆ ◆

Happy Father's Day

CHAPTER 22

ARE YOU A CUT ABOVE THE REST?

I have always been a fan of quizzes and played the question master on many occasions. Here is my butchery quiz with some of my favourite questions to test your knowledge.

QUIZ

1.   What is a bath chap?
2.   In butchers' back slang what is a Gel bee-mal?
3.   At what age does a sheep become mutton?
4.   From what animal does a nice bit of skirt come from?
5.   What is the traditional way to cook pig's trotters?
6.   What are the thymus and pancreas glands more commonly known as?
7.   What is Biltong?
8.   In which month does National Butchers' Week fall?
9.   Breast of lamb, belly of pork ……?…. of beef
10.   After the war, what year did meat rationing end?
11.   A cushion of lamb is made from which part of the animal?
12.   What is a 'poussin'?
13.   What is a 'leveret'?
14.   The grouse shooting season starts on which date?
15.   What are the two main ingredients of faggots?
16.   What are steelyards used for?
17.   What is the only part of the pig you cannot eat?
18.   The sirloin of beef was so named by which English monarch?
19.   How many grams equal one lb.?
20.   What is traditionally served on January the 25th each year?

Answers: Back page.

CHAPTER 23

THE FUTURE

If I had said to my Father forty years ago, when I started in the business, that we would now be selling kangaroo, bison, wild boar and crocodile, he would have said, "you're off your rocker son."

Who knows what the next 40 years will bring? Will we be just popping a pill into our mouth as a supplement for food? Let's hope not, as one of the pleasures in life is the taste of different meats.

A nice joint of belly pork with crackling, a well hung rib-eye steak, the smell of bacon being cooked, enough to make your mouth water. The only thing that is certain is one day the ownership of any business must change. I see myself as the current custodian, until the time is right for the next generation to take over. However, I'm intending to stay around for a good few years yet, health permitting. Five, ten, twenty years when the time is right my son Billy will take over. He is very passionate about our business, and though not hands on at the moment, he has contributed in his own way to the running of the business. 88% of current family business owners believe the same family or families will control their business in five years, but succession statistics undermine this belief. Only about 30% of family businesses survive into the second generation, and only about 3% of all family businesses operate into the fourth generation or beyond. So, being a 26th generation butcher in our family business makes us quite unique.

A day in the life of a good butcher is a busy one, and it is a remarkable achievement that we have been in business for 500 years. As statistics show, too many family firms fail to successfully pass from generation to generation, so we have been fortunate to do so.

One of the best things about being in a family business, is the control you have over your own destiny, and although we are the oldest, it is more important to strive to be the best.

For us it is all about the quality of the product and the personal service we offer our customers, many of whom represent families, who have been customers for generations. It's about the here and now and planning to succeed. We have a long history, but every generation needs to build on what's been handed down to them, and more importantly be prepared for long hours and plenty of hard work. This will provide the opportunity to reap and enjoy the benefits of being your own boss and in control of your own destiny.

However, nothing is certain in life. You only get out from any business what you put in. You have got to be in the shop, hands on, in full command of your ship. You have to build a trusting relationship with your customers. This, you can only earn over a period of time. I'm not sure I will ever retire, it will be nice to be like Father, and ease back gradually, at the same time keeping an eye on things. Father was well into his 80s when he decided to cut back a little on the manual work. However, his knowledge and book keeping skills were invaluable. It was reassuring that Father was there with a life time of wisdom and support if needed. It is great to have someone to turn to in an hour of need, and again I count myself very lucky to have had such a long working relationship with my father.

I'm so grateful for the knowledge and expertise Father handed down to me. He placed his trust in me to carry on the business, and it has been a privilege to succeed him, and be part of our butchery history, and 500 years behind the block. I look forward to the day when I can offer my son the same guidance.

THE END

◆ ◆ ◆ ◆ ◆ ◆

Billy Balson

QUIZ ANSWERS

1.	Cooked pig's cheek		11.	Shoulder
2.	Leg of lamb		12.	Small Chicken
3.	Two years		13.	Young Hare
4.	Cow		14.	12th August
5.	Boiled		15.	Pork and Liver
6.	Sweetbreads		16.	Weighing
7.	Air dried beef or game		17.	Squeak
8.	March		18.	Henry VIII
9.	Brisket		19.	454 grams
10.	1954		20.	Haggis

HOW DID YOU SCORE?

1-10 NOVICE
MUST TRY HARDER

11-15 NOT BAD
COULD DO BETTER

16-19 WELL DONE
GOOD CARNIVOROUS UNDERSTANDING

20 EXCELLENT
A GREAT FOOD CONNOISSEUR

PLEASE APPLY FOR THE NEXT JOB AT
R J BALSON & SON